CLINGING TO THE CRAGS

CLINGING *to the* CRAGS

Also by Katharine Grant

WRITING AS KATHARINE GRANT

Sedition (2014)

WRITING AS K.M. GRANT

de Granville Trilogy
Blood Red Horse (2004)
Green Jasper (2005)
Blaze of Silver (2007)

Perfect Fire Trilogy
Blue Flame (2008)
White Heat (2008)
Paradise Red (2009)

Novels
How the Hangman Lost His Heart (2006)
Belle's Song (2010)
Hartslove (2011)

CLINGING to the CRAGS

KATHARINE GRANT

SALT

CROMER

PUBLISHED BY SALT PUBLISHING 2026

2 4 6 8 10 9 7 5 3 1

Copyright © Katharine Grant 2026

Katharine Grant has asserted her right under the Copyright, Designs
and Patents Act 1988 to be identified as the author of this work.

First published in Great Britain in 2026 by
Salt Publishing Ltd
12 Norwich Road, Cromer, Norfolk NR27 0AX, United Kingdom

GPSR representative
Matt Parsons matt.parsons@upi2mbooks.hr
UPI-2M PLUS d.o.o., Medulićeva 20, 10000 Zagreb, Croatia

www.saltpublishing.com

Salt Publishing Limited Reg. No. 5293401

A CIP catalogue record for this book is available from the British Library

ISBN 978 1 78463 389 9 (Paperback edition)
ISBN 978 1 78463 397 4 (Electronic edition)

Typeset in Neacademia by Salt Publishing

Printed and bound in Great Britain by Clays Ltd, Elcograf S.p.A.

for Joan, Paula and Brian,
and never forgetting Mrs. Nicks

GENEALOGY

**This family tree is heavily abbreviated.
Only those mentioned in this memoir are included.**

many previous generations of Towneleys of Towneley

Charles Towneley
1803-1876   m   **Caroline Harriet Molyneux**
1803-1866

Caroline Theresa 1838-1873

m

Montagu Bertie, Lord Norreys
later 7th Earl of Abingdon 1836-1928

Emily Frances 1839-1892

m

Lord Alexander Gordon-Lennox
1825-1892

Alice Mary 1846-1921

m

Lord O'Hagan 1812-1885

Lady Alice Josephine Bertie 1865-1950

m

1.Sir Gerald Portal 1858-1894
2. **Major Robert Reyntiens 1853-1913**

Cosmo Gordon-Lennox
1868-1921

two sons
two daughters

Priscilla Reyntiens 1899-1991

m

1. Colonel Alexander Koch de Gooreynd 1899-1985
divorced 1929

m

2. Lord Norman 1871-1950
(Montagu Norman, Governor of the Bank of England)

Sir Simon Towneley KCVO
1921-2022

Sir Peregrine Worsthorne
1923-2020

m

Mary Fitzherbert
1935-2001

Eldest Sister b 1956	Second Sister b 1957	me b 1958	Only Brother b1962	Fourth Sister b 1964	Fifth Sister b 1967	Sixth Sister b1969

1

AM I DEAD?

'AM I DEAD?' asked my father the morning of the day he died. 'I don't think so,' said Fourth Sister, resisting the urge to say 'try harder', which was what my father would have said had roles been reversed. As it was, she propped up his pillows and gave him a cup of tea. 'At least if you are, we all are.' My father humphed.

'He seemed both pleased and cross to find himself still here,' Fourth Sister said a little later. My siblings and I were downstairs in the kitchen, trying to work out why the gas oven seemed to have melted all its knobs. The Aga was for cooking. The gas oven was used only for toast. I don't know why we never got a toaster. We just didn't. 'Do you think he's actually dying?' asked one of us, perhaps me, perhaps Fifth Sister, or even Sixth. No matter. It was The Question. We all considered.

For dinner the previous evening our father had asked for soup, partridge in cream and two glasses of champagne, more the 'fuck you' final dinner of a man facing the gallows than the last hurrah of a man nearly 101 and still busy with the final volume of Chips Channon's diaries. On the other hand, the priest had given him the Last Rites and our father wasn't a multiple Last Rites kind of person.

One of us said 'Let's go and see.' So we trooped out of the kitchen, past the pantry, through the door to the front, up the stairs, passed my mother's sitting room and my father's library, up another set of stairs, and then another, then along the passage past the Rose Room, down more stairs and along another passage to where my father lay in the narrow wooden bed in which my great-grandmother had died seventy-two years before. It would be a long and hazardous trip for the undertaker.

My father wasn't reading. He wanted to hear the hymn 'Lead Kindly Light'. With sly malice, the house randomly thwarted the internet, so we scrambled for a hymn book. Fourth Sister began:

> Lead, Kindly Light, amidst th'encircling gloom,
> Lead Thou me on!
> The night is dark, and I am far from home,
> Lead Thou me on!
>
> . . .
>
> So long Thy power hath blest me, sure it still
> Will lead me on.
> O'er moor and fen, o'er crag and torrent, till
> The night is gone,
> And with the morn those angel faces smile,
> Which I have loved long since, and lost awhile!

There are moments in those hours waiting for death that pierce, moments when, without the intrusion of the mundane – counting pills, changing water, tidying a blanket, emptying a commode – what you're witnessing would overwhelm. We grit our teeth, don't we, to get through those moments, feeling the focus should be on the dying. We, the still living, have time. We never know how much time, but more time, it's reasonable to assume, than the person whose pills we're counting.

For me, that hymn was such a moment. There was, of course, the natural sadness at the fading out of a parent. Yet there was more.

How to explain? My father was a firm believer in male primogeniture. He'd always been clear that although the estate he'd inherited was neither large nor prosperous, when he died, however many daughters he had, the estate would go to his oldest son. His only son, as it turned out. The Boy. We girls might love the place but our gender made our stake in it fleeting. Whilst our father lived, it was still our home even if we had a house elsewhere complete with husband and children. Once he'd gone, as daughters we'd be gone too. As I say, I'd always known this, so it was hardly a new grief. Nonetheless, something in that hymn, maybe the mention of 'moors, fens, crags and torrents', hit me like a slamming door. My father's death was more than one death. From his last breath, in the place I loved best in the world I'd be reduced to a visitor. From that moment, if I wanted to return I'd have to be invited. I know, I know. Amid all the world's horrors, being relegated from rooted fixture to invited visitor is less than nothing. And anyway, being married for forty years and settled in Scotland, wasn't I a visitor already?

But we're strange creatures, we humans. Over some things we're fools and continue to be fools no matter where our foolishness leads or how it pains. There was nothing unexpected about my father's death, nothing unexpected about what would happen afterwards, yet now I was sitting by his deathbed, my whole being felt precarious. Untethered, unanchored, I gripped the sides of my chair. Only Brother, sitting by the window, seemed oblivious. Fathers die. Sons inherit. Isn't that just the way of things? Had a gun been handy I might have murdered him.

Fourth Sister's voice fell away, and in a rare admission of fear my father took her hand. I let go of my chair. Never mind what was coming after. Now I, like the others, was praying, and praying urgently, for that 'kindly light' to banish the fear and lead my father on to his eternal rest.

Had we been living in a novel, I suppose my father would have sighed and died, or at least miraculously acquired the patience he'd so conspicuously lacked in life and surrendered himself entirely to the will of God. In fact, after a moment or two he let go of Fourth Sister's hand and asked who was reading Robert Harris's *Act of Oblivion*, lying on the table at which, the evening before, he'd eaten his partridge. 'I am,' said Only Brother.

'Isn't there a poem about the execution of Charles I? Was it Marlowe?'

'Not Marlowe—'

'Of course not Marlowe!' snapped my father. 'Quite the wrong date. Andrew Marvell. Could you get it?'

Again a scramble, this time for a poetry anthology. Only Brother read the poem.

'What terrible diction you have,' said my father.

The day passed into evening. He lay half impatient – what was death doing, taking so long? – and half comforted by two whippets, two labradors and a terrier, a pack of canine Charons all dozing but ready, when called, to ferry him to the underworld. The District Nurse came and left paperwork which, though she didn't exactly say, made it clear that she didn't expect to return in my father's lifetime. At around 8 p.m., my father said 'I think you should all go downstairs and have dinner'. He asked if one of us would stay. We knew he wanted Sixth Sister. A brief stint as a veterinary nurse meant she was his fount of all things medical into which category death, I suppose, falls. We'd barely got down the stairs before we were summoned back. He'd gone.

'Let it go or it'll kill you' was the advice of a cousin who, along with her sisters, had been through more or less the same male primogeniture distress. I can't let go, though, without capturing how it was, how we were. In this gathering, a not strictly chronological chronicle, lies my claim not of right but of love.

I've shown none of my siblings this account. As a wise obituaries editor once told me, families make troublesome collaborators. Recollections always differ. Differ they may but I don't believe in the weaselly concept of 'my truth'. There is truth; there is also recollection, reminiscence, artistic licence, conflation, inflation, getting it wrong and getting carried away. A memoir contains all these things. All these things are here.

2

CLINGING TO
THE CRAGS

1969

THE FIRST TIME I ran away from home I was eleven and took with me my wicked dog, the flat cap I prayed might magically turn me into a boy, and *Wuthering Heights*. Dog, cap, the book I was currently inhabiting. Perhaps I took an apple. I climbed the couple of miles or so up the moor to the ruins of what had been a lead mine. Sheltered by a broken wall, moors in front, moors behind, moors to each side, I realised with a stab of what I took then to be disappointment but now recognise as something quite different, that I didn't want to run away. I didn't want to go anywhere else at all. What I really wanted was for somebody to miss me. I went through the list: parents, siblings, nanny, nurserymaid, Mrs N., cook, gardener.

My parents - unlikely. With seven children and the sole boy the only one of much interest, my father would have to be reminded which of his six daughters I was. My mother, eternally (so it seemed to me) pregnant, was fed up with children. She might have been happier had we all vanished. My siblings themselves, well . . .

Oldest Sister - sent to boarding school aged seven and now fourteen, she was quite lofty in those days. She might not remember I existed.

Second Sister – eighteen months older than me, we looked so alike we could impersonate each other. She'd probably pretend to be me and assume all my things as her own. I didn't like the thought of that.

Me – I was Third Child.

Only Brother – three years younger than me and of a Pollyanna-ish disposition, he'd carry on smiling even if I turned up as a corpse. 'Never mind!' he'd say, 'plenty of other sisters!'

Fourth Sister – she would think it was a pity, but really, older sisters are interchangeable.

The Little Ones, as Fifth and Sixth Sister were called long after they were Big Ones, would have welcomed my departure. About a decade separated us and I wasn't kind to them. Why should they miss me?

Mrs N. would be too busy singing as she polished things both polishable and unpolishable or, on hands and knees with brush and bucket, scoured the flags at the back door. How she loved those flags!

The cook would be shouting 'shut the bloody doors' either in English or Italian, depending on the cook, as she tried to persuade the bread to rise despite the kitchen being designed to prevent it.

The gardener would just say 'reet, well . . .' and carry on digging or mowing or pretending to eat worms.

This left Nanny who, in any case, was the most likely because she had a vested interest: losing a child might possibly, although not certainly, mean dismissal without a reference. A small gamble, it was nonetheless a gamble she might not want to take.

Eventually, realising that the risk of not being missed by anybody was the biggest risk of all, and feeling aggrieved and silly in equal measure, I secured my cap, trapped Heathcliff and Catherine Earnshaw back between book covers, pretended that my dog had come nicely to heel, and turned down the hill towards home.

It's strange. When people ask you about home, they always ask where you were born when the question that really fixes home isn't about your birthplace at all. It's about where you want to end up either buried or scattered. I feel sad for people who say, 'I don't care,

I'll be dead'. Death is cold enough, even colder without the warmth of rootedness. Your ending-up-place doesn't have to be a specific spot – it could be the sea. It's just somewhere to land, somewhere you'll be welcomed, absorbed, folded in.

Long after my running-away-day, it struck me that by trudging up the moor rather than down to the village, or to the bus-stop, or to the road to cadge a lift, I had unwittingly asked and answered my own ending-up question. And my answer has never altered. I want to end up – it'll have to be ashes – folded into the rough edge of the high moor that links, intermittently, the haunts of the Pendle witches with the Brontës' restless imaginings. My spot is between Stonehouse Cottage and Cowside Farm, underneath, or next to, my mother's memorial stone.

It can be bleak up there but what with the birds, foxes, badgers and sheep, I'll hardly be alone. There's the farmer checking his stock; the dumper dumping his rust-bucket; the cyclists, riders, walkers and runners toiling along the forty-eight-mile circular loop, named after my mother – part of the national trail along the spine of England for which she fought and won. At her memorial stone, toilers are exhorted to pause and allow the 'wild and romantic terrain of the Pennine Bridleway' to refresh the spirit – a happy euphemism for catching your breath. It's steep country. Heart-attack country. Good country to die in.

If you haven't died and are facing downhill, to your left you'll see Burnley, developed or exploited, depending on your point of view, by the industrial revolution for industrial purposes. Water was Burnley's making, the rivers Calder and Brun driving looms weaving cotton, with mills, foundries and ironworks straddling the banks of the Leeds/Liverpool canal – 'muck mekin brass'. And there was coal, with Bank Hall's gantries, chimneys and winding towers rising like fairground attractions from the dark sprawl of service buildings. When I was small, the mills and pit pulsed with less conviction but were still familiar elements in the town's silhouette. At night, the patchwork sweep of neon lights offered a passable imitation of the Bay of Naples, or so my father always said as we swept along the road above Burnley, heading home in the car. 'The Bay of Naples' we would echo and suddenly be transported, the car almost lifting, flying us to Naples, until we crashed back to earth when the lights disappeared.

At the road junction, most people turned left towards the town. We turned right. Burnley was our town but we were embedded – the right word, I think, being deeper than 'lived' – some miles away in the mouth of a gorge, sometimes more and sometimes less valleyed, gouged by glacial erosion during the last ice-age. Inhabitants of more chocolate-box country may be disconcerted to find brindled cliffs occasionally closing like mismatched jaws above the slim spine of a road which feels, in parts, too flimsy to wedge the jaws apart. If the jaws snapped shut, you'd be pressed against the ghosts of the small mines, mainly drift – Copy, Railway, Cliviger, Union – whose engine houses and pumping stations once shuttled coal along ginny tracks to main collection points. The gorge is steep but not uninhabited. Broken lines of terraced houses protrude like bad teeth, each house roughly the width of two coffins, longwise. What kind of people live with their front windows against the road and their backs against a cliff? Most people never discover. They're just relieved, after four or so miles, to be disgorged.

Why not find a smudge of layby and stop. Get out. Never mind the dead fridges, splintered televisions and other shit both real and metaphorical. Never mind the wind. Squint against the rain (it's bound to be raining) and imagine the days before coal gash and smelting works, before tanneries and foundries, before tarmac and roadsigns, before those bad-teeth houses, the days when above and around was only bog and bosk and the rush of water down the cloughs. The wind you're cursing now is the same wind, albeit a little sullied, and the river, despite some discolouration and the chill cast by rocky overhangs, is a picnic river with stepping stones. Nippy, naturally, with all that tumbling water, but a lovely gush against the legs.

If the cloud allows, look up, and between low water and high moor you'll see farms clinging to crags, and drystone walls tracing fields that nature has shaped. There are larks and curlews, rising and rising – even the sheep seem to rise. What sentient creature can resist the gorge's primeval pull, the anti-gravitational imperative to climb to the top? And at the top, spread before you, the untrammelled, unadorned grey-green moor. The wind blows differently up here. If you're riding, your horse's mane will whip your nose; if you're walking, your wet coat will slap-flap against your legs.

For me, the wind-whip and slap-flap is the feel of home. Our father owned (or our family had owned, or nobody was sure who owned, or nobody wanted to own) the land which was our play-ground, so beyond the house and the garden my siblings and I roamed as we pleased. Our world was boundless. More than the world. On top of the moor, the universe seemed ours.

Once we could stay on our ponies, our universe expanded. We could choose a known way up the moor or an unknown. We could hitch up our stirrups, pretend we were jockeys aboard Kettledrum, our family's 1861 Derby winner, and gallop wildly across terrain only fit for walking. We could pull over railway sleepers and run our own Grand National round the reservoir tracks. We could let down our stirrups and pretend to be auditioning for the Spanish Riding School. We could just ride, sometimes facing forward or daring each other to face backwards. Our ponies put up with us or dumped us as the mood took them. An hour, a day, who was counting? We barely noticed the cold. It was nearly always wet. There was only one constraint – there's always one. Ours was hunger. Stomachs are so confining. Otherwise, we vanished and nobody missed us.

This freedom was a treasure but it wasn't a gift. Gifts are considered and chosen. Our freedom was neither. It was just how my parents were, my mother nearly always distracted and my father unaware that children were creatures you might worry about. Wise nannies take their cue from their employers. In that respect, all our nannies were wise. After all, no child died, and any child who ran away always came back for tea.

So it was that at teatime, sheepish and hungry, I scrambled and slid down the moor up which I had stridden less than two hours before. Why couldn't I be more like Catherine Earnshaw? She certainly wouldn't have been looking forward to macaroni cheese. She'd have been shaking her hair and dissolving into the mist. 'Cathy' (I felt we were on first-name terms) 'would have no time for me,' I told my dog although he wasn't the listening sort. Feeling utterly discouraged – why wasn't I somebody else? – I left the moor behind and scuffed along the stony track. In roughly ten minutes, I was lifting the latch of the meadow gate and standing at the top of the garden facing the spread of the house. It was a long spread, some windows curtained with heavy Italian silk, others tightly shuttered, as though the house itself couldn't decide whether to welcome me in or keep me out.

How best to effect re-entry? Should I creep through the back and pretend I'd never run away? Should I make a bigger entrance? Fantasy land! An entire cohort of trumpeting angels wouldn't galvanise a welcoming party of open arms. I must say at once that I didn't feel unloved. It was just that my parents' love was expressed more easily at the end of letters than in hugs. Certainly, it was never to be either demonstrated or expressed in Nanny's hearing. Love was a private thing, not to be cheapened by public declaration.

I skirted the house. Front door? Garden door? North door? Back door? None would be locked so I wouldn't have to knock, though that didn't diminish the humiliation of a failed runaway. In the end, I chose the north door. In my mind it was the home of the North Wind whose laugh was 'like the breaking of silver bubbles'.[*] Also, dishearteningly mundane, I'd left my indoor shoes next to the croquet set that lived behind it. The second time I ran

* MacDonald, George (1871), *At the Back of the North Wind*, Strahan & Co., London

away from home was no more successful. After that, I gave up
running away and focused on my real ambition - never to leave
at all.

3

IMPOSTER SYNDROME

So, WHO WERE we, we seven siblings raised in the Victorian nursery of a many-doored house embedded on the edge of a valley gorge near Burnley. We were not fashionable people because northeast Lancashire isn't, and has never been, a place for fashionable people. Northeast Lancashire is like the 'fly over' states in the USA: people swish through on the M6 noting only the names of towns they don't want to visit and landscape they don't like the look of. Remember the JAM's song 'It's grim up north'? Burnley is the fifth town on their long grim list.

Perhaps the 'swish through' and the grimness is why we didn't think our childhood odd. We lived in an odd, grim place, so why shouldn't an upbringing be a generation or two out of date? Visitors were disappointed. Northern grimness should at least mean a hardscrabble lineage of miners or mill-workers. It was thoroughly disconcerting, almost outrageous, that in this odd, grim place there should be a grand(ish) family clinging to grander times – a bit like being offered scuffed ballet flats when you expected serviceable clogs. Yet that was us, the scuffed ballet flats, clinging on. And clinging on with us were the nannies, the nurserymaids, and a Sicilian butler, Carmello, trained by my father, his uniform buttons polished to dazzle. It was the work of many to keep our geographically isolated, socially unfashionable and increasingly archaic show on the road.

Quite simply, we were what remained of the Towneleys, a once very grand northern family of recusant Catholics, in other words Catholics who had remained Catholic when it was neither wise nor strategic. Everything Towneley had filtered down to us through the female line, so there were complications. For my father, it had been quite a bumpy ride. Born Simon Koch de Gooreynd, he became Simon Worsthorne, then Simon Towneley Worsthorne, and only finally, and by Royal Licence on his wedding day, Towneley. Unlike their wives, not many bridegrooms enter the church called one thing and emerge called something else.

Bumpy rides notwithstanding, being Simon Towneley dictated how my father viewed the world and how he wanted the world to view him. According to the historian Dr. Whitaker, although the first mention of 'Tunleia' is during the reign of King John, the family that became Towneley lived in Lancashire – at what eventually became Towneley Hall – from around the year 871. Richard Towneley represented Lancashire at the court of Edward III; Towneleys fought at Agincourt. A long family tree lists heroes and villains, the degenerate and the dashing, the important and importunate. Central to it all was that resolute Catholicism. *Tenez Le Vrai* (hold to the truth) was the Towneley motto. My father never forgot it. We were expected to live up to it.

Usually on the wrong, or at least the losing, side when it mattered, in the civil war the Towneleys championed the king. Charles Towneley was killed at Marston Moor and when Mary Towneley braved the battlefield to reclaim his body, she was kindly treated by an officer afterwards identified as Oliver Cromwell. This tale so moved a Rochdale bus driver that for years, on the battle's July anniversary he would ride his cranky old horse up our stable drive in full seventeenth century fig to bring my mother, another Mary Towneley, 'news of your husband's demise'.

'Good sir, terrible news indeed.' Even on the Cavalier's first visit my mother wasn't disconcerted. Still girlishly slim – nobody could believe she'd had seven children – when wielding a mucking-out fork she had the look of a World War Two land-girl, a look she never lost, just as she never lost her gift for launching straight into the unlikely.

The Cavalier, immersed in his part, didn't blink.

'I shall take you to him,' he said and leant over as if to sweep her onto his saddle. Some days, I think she'd have gladly gone, regardless that he in his full seventeenth century fig and she in her most un-seventeenth century jodhpurs would have made an outlandish pair. Some days, she might even have thought news of a husband's demise wasn't so terrible. We all have those kinds of days. It's only luck that a Cavalier doesn't always turn up.

But on this first and all subsequent occasions, my mother hopped neatly to one side. 'Let the dead take care of themselves. You have ridden a long way.'

'From Rochdale,' said the Cavalier.

'Rochdale is far,' said my mother, though it wasn't really. 'Come. Dine and sleep, both you and your horse.'

So every year, they did.

My father, though less keen on the Cavalier, and surprised to find he took his claret with a lump or two of sugar, was still keen to acknowledge our forbears. He had three favourites. There was John Towneley (died 1608), imprisoned during the Reformation for refusing to conform to the new order. Another John collected books. And not just any books. Until sold to finance the restructuring of Towneley Hall, John's library was one of the finest in England. Amongst other jewels, he acquired a set of medieval mystery plays, and in 1804 bought what became known as the Towneley Lectionary, originally created for Cardinal Alessandro Farnese and illuminated by Giulio Clovio. The price was £400. John's nephew Charles (died 1805) was the celebrated collector of antiquities, including the Graeco-Roman marbles famously painted by Zoffany. When Charles died, the marbles were bought by the British Museum and formed a core collection.

As children, we naturally much preferred hanged, drawn and quartered Uncle Frank Towneley, a lock of whose hair was encased in a small leather frame on a little table in the drawing room. And of course our Derby hero Kettledrum, on whom it was said Pope Pius IX had placed a little bet. We nodded to Richard Towneley, inventor of deadbeat escapement, a mechanism none of us understood. Richard also recorded rainfall. In north-east Lancashire, we understood that very well. From all this you can perhaps see that no matter the complications, Towneley was a good name to end up with.

So, it was sad that despite all the courage and distinction, God didn't reward the Towneleys with a steady crop of heirs. Instead, in the early 1880s, after losing three male heirs in three years, the name vanished and the whole estate was broken up. Charles Towneley's (yet another Charles) oldest daughter Caroline, married to Montagu Bertie, seventh Earl of Abingdon, had died in 1873. The Cliviger land and farms went to Emily, Charles' second daughter, married to Lord Alexander Gordon-Lennox, and she, in turn, left her portion to her son, Cosmo Gordon-Lennox. Charles' third daughter, Alice, married to Lord O'Hagan, got Towneley Hall – aka 'the Grand House' – with the surrounding park, and promptly sold the whole kit and kaboodle to the Burnley council. Emily's son Cosmo – exotic, childless, and who never set foot in Lancashire – left everything he inherited to his first cousin, Lady Alice Josephine Bertie, always known as 'Joey', daughter of the dead Caroline. Confused? We were. On the one hand, we were Towneleys and we'd been around in Lancashire forever. On the other, after name changes, deaths, deed polls, Royal Licences and the sale of the Grand House, we weren't really Towneleys at all. My father decided enough was enough. Despite female lines and the loss of the Grand House, the family had survived. Family trumps all. There would be a Towneley restoration.

Very late in life and with the frankness of old age, my father revealed another reason, possibly less commendable but more accurate, for embracing the Towneley mantle: he couldn't think of anything else to do. He'd returned from the war, then volunteered, or perhaps 'was volunteered' for the 1946 Allied Mission to Observe the Greek Elections, after which he returned to Oxford, wrote a book on seventeenth century Venetian opera and became a music don.

'I don't know why I became a don,' he confided as he approached his hundredth birthday. 'I hated teaching.'

'Why didn't you go into banking or some money kind of job?' It seemed a logical question for a man whose stepfather had been the Governor of the Bank of England. And a harmless question except that my father viewed all questions, whether existential or mundane, as traps deliberately set to catch him out. Any glimmer of an upward inflection and he whipped the question round and snapped its teeth on the questioner. Perhaps he harboured a grudge against answers. In any event, he seldom gave one, at least to his children. When people told us our father knew a lot about gardens and music and the like, we took their word for it. He didn't welcome enquiries of any kind from us. I knew, then, that his head would snap up.

It snapped up. 'Money people. What do such people do?'

'I don't know,' I said, unsure if the snapping was over.

Then, 'me neither,' he said, 'so what good would I have been?'

Relief made me brave. 'I expect somebody would have told you what to do.'

A look of utter horror crossed his face, as though I'd suggested taking instruction from a devil-worshipper. 'I suppose they would. Thank goodness it never came to that.'

It was never going to 'come to that'. Since he'd spent much of his childhood in Lancashire with his maternal grandmother, and since the portion of the estate that she'd inherited was entailed to him, he already had somewhere to go. The 'job' of restoration involved neither students nor instruction from devil-worshippers, so what was there to decide?

It was a long time before I thought of my father as a 'restorer'. To me, he was continuity. He was a Towneley. We were Towneleys. Towneleys belonged here. It was our place. I did, on occasion, wonder why my father's mother, our grandmother, was a Norman; why our father's father was a Koch de Gooreynd, and why my father's brother was a Worsthorne, but since no explanation was offered, it didn't seem to matter much. More pressing for a child with the Towneley name was its variety of spellings.

When each successive child left primary school, my parents gave two volumes of the Encyclopaedia Britannica to the school library. To complete the school's collection, my mother would have needed to produce at least a dozen children, so I'm not sure what she made of this present. Anyhow, being child three, my volumes were five and six, and on school-leaving day I had to inscribe them with my signature. My father's glowering presence, the gravity of writing in a published book, the responsibility of an actual signature and the awful threat of ink blots sat very heavy. Under the weight I experienced a sudden and terrible blank about the number of 'e's' in the name of which we were told to be so proud. Townley? Towneley? Toweneley? But I had to sign right then, and what kind of idiot has to ask their father how to spell their own name? My father was not kind to idiots. He was also waiting, and he wasn't patient. In a flash of inspiration, I remembered that our ancestors, perhaps in a similar crisis, had inserted and removed e's just as they pleased, so I signed one book Katharine Townley after Charles Townley the antiquarian, and the other Katharine Towneley after John Towneley the book collector. I screwed the lid on my pen (no blots) and stepped back. My father stepped forward, blinked, peered, froze. In the icy silence I inserted the missing 'e'. Names can be messy.

I think now that my father found the Towneley hereditary manoeuvrings humiliating. He envied our near neighbours, the Tempests, their unbroken continuity, if not father to son, then at least male to male. No dribbling down through the female line at Broughton Hall; no added or missing e's' in Tempest; and unlike us, their ancestral pile wasn't now owned by the council and turned into a museum and art gallery. Broughton might have been the coldest house in England – in those days you had to surprise the boiler for hot water – but the Tempests still lived in it. It was their home.

'Do you mind about Towneley?' It was years before I plucked up the courage to ask my father this obvious question about our erstwhile Grand House. We were driving to Broughton for a Tempest funeral, passing Towneley's rather sad gatehouse, with Unity College, one of those buildings inspired by a cardboard box, parked behind and a bathroom showroom opposite. Only a couple of miles by road from the rather less grand house in which my great-grandmother had lived and was now our home, Towneley was very familiar to us. 'Are you sad we don't live there?'

I expected a snipsnap. But the Broughton funeral, both he and I dressed in deep black and me clutching a mantilla, had softened him, or perhaps, for a moment, he thought I was somebody else. 'An estate that loses its house loses its centre,' he said in a voice as sad as the gatehouse.

'Do you find it painful to visit? To take visitors down and show them around?' Being so close to home, showing visitors round the lost Grand House, with its story-book long gallery, its shivery priest-hole and the chapel in which every year on All Souls Day we prayed for all the Towneley dead, was a familiar routine.

My father glanced over and realised it was me. Now came the snipsnap. 'We're not imposters, if that's what you mean.'

'That's not what I asked,' I might have said. I didn't. Anyway, I don't know why he was so prickly. We weren't imposters. The family tree told us that. But I suppose when you inherit through the female line and dedicate your whole life to the nebulous concept of restoration you are something, and you don't have to be an imposter to suffer from imposter syndrome.

For myself, though I've suffered imposter syndrome over many things, I've never suffered from it as a Towneley. Nor was my attachment to the Grand House as sadly regretful as my father's. My siblings and I had plans and they were quite simple: we'd buy the house and park back from the council, restore both to the glories Turner painted circa 1798, and live grandly 'at home' forever and ever. The public would still be allowed in but instead of being a museum filled with museum things, it would be filled with us.

This unhealthy dream might have dwindled had it not been that then, as now, when you visit Towneley its past inhabitants hover on the other side of the panelling and at the turn of the stairs. Is that silhouette Peregrine Towneley (died 1846), whose clothes were so rough he was sometimes mistaken for a poacher? Are those the shades of Towneley girls still dancing? Is that Great-x-3 Aunt Alice grinding the stubs of her cheroots into the drawing room's polished floor?

So we planned, plotted and schemed: thefts, heists or luck with the premium bonds for the money: sit-ins, occupations or plain old conquest to re-establish our presence. Could we do both things – money and presence – simultaneously by dressing up as Towneleys past, but not to us entirely gone? If we lived as them, might people pay for the spectacle? Would they pay enough for us, the present Towneleys, to keep the past Towneleys alive and resplendent? We were always heartened when, on inspecting the family tree, visitors to Towneley asked about us, listed at the bottom, 'Gee, are they still alive?' It was delightful to 'out' yourself – 'that's me!' It was also delightful not to out yourself and float about feeling ghostly.

So, fantasist Towneleys yes. Imposter Towneleys no. We children were quite clear on that. As for my father, both fantasy and imposter paled beside his real fear, a fear that never vanished, a fear that absolutely ruled his life, and by extension ours.

4

SLIPPERY SLOPE

WHEN YOU'RE LITTLE, you don't much think about slippery slopes except those which involve mud or snow. My father's slippery slope involved neither. To him, the slippery slope was all to do with the *ne plus ultra* of terrors: change. Change, so he believed, set in motion a downward slither. Give change any quarter and its velocity would increase. Within minutes, we'd be swept away, and with us what remained of the beautiful things collected by Towneleys over centuries, so many of which had, when the Grand House was sold, already been plucked from their settled spaces and tossed hither and thither like birds in a storm. In other words, if we didn't want to be propelled, helter-skelter, towards the utter catastrophe of a last Towneley hurrah, change must be resisted. To my father, change wasn't just frightening, it was frightful.

The frontline of the war against change was the house in which we lived, the Not-So-Grand house originally built for the agent responsible for the part of the estate left to my great-grandmother and which she eventually made her home. It's said that she 'persuaded' the agent to leave. I wonder about 'persuasion'. One person's 'persuasion' is often another's 'booting out'. Whatever, he went, and since this persuasive booting happened long before my time, whatever our fantasies about the Grand House, when I think of home I think of the Not-So-Grand house in which we were born, from which we never moved, and in which, because of my father's slippery slope phobia, nothing much else moved either. However uncomfortable and inconvenient, in the Not-So-Grand house everything was suspended, stuck more or less exactly as it was in my great-grandmother's time, cemented in place by my father's implacable mantra 'if it was good enough for my grandmother, it's good enough for you'. In other words, 'no more slippage'.

The Not-So-Grand house was not beautiful. My own grandmother, my father's mother, was appalled at her first vision of the frowning black stone, the glowering black-framed windows, the three black gables separated by two dark and ominous valley gutters – valley gutters in the Land of Rain! – the whole thing dug into such a vertiginous slope that carelessly parked cars rattled downwards to oblivion. Who could possibly have built this 'suburban villa on a bleak hillside' she asked. The answer was my Great-x-2 grandfather, the Earl of Abingdon. He himself lived in beautiful Wytham Abbey in Oxfordshire. To him, an unbeautiful suburban villa was exactly the kind of house that an agent in the industrial north looking after the remnants of a once-great estate should live in. He can't have imagined for one minute that anybody to whom he was related would settle there. Absolutely impossible to believe that war, fate and circumstance could conspire so that one of the settlers would be his own daughter. Yet that's what happened. With two dead husbands and no intention of trying a third, my great-grandmother arrived in 1921. Within months she had grafted herself onto her mother's Towneley roots so deeply that when she (my great-grandmother) died in 1950 many people assumed that despite the Grand House down the road, she'd lived in the Not-So-Grand house forever.

Uncompromising, spiky, a little forbidding – I'm talking about the Not-So-Grand house, though by all accounts the description equally fits my great-grandmother – the front of the house is defended by four steep and slithery steps. No bar or balustrade offers a helpful bolster against a potentially fatal tumble. If you do manage to ascend without incident you must twist the iron handle of the thick, wooden, iron-bolted front door and push pretty hard before, with a kind of grumpy grunt not unlike a cow giving birth, the door opens to let you and many draughts inside. There you're presented with a house of, essentially, passages with rooms attached. In the passages, monstrous iron radiators occasionally belch out heat. The rooms themselves, apart from those with real fires, are completely unheated and in our childhoods even electric fires were difficult since most rooms had, and some still have, only one plug, a tiny round pin affair that went out of fashion in about 1947. There is, of course, inside plumbing. Mysteriously, though, the water which washes liberally down the hill and gushes into the domestic tank emerges through the taps only as a shy dribble, or no dribble at all if more than one tap runs at once. Unless the roof leaks in just the right spot sometimes you can barely fill a lukewarm toothmug in under twenty minutes. Yet even the gentlest observation that this didn't really constitute plumbing provoked a paroxysm in my father. If you could say an entire rosary in the time a bath took to run at least there had been no slippage.

With a son arriving after the birth of three daughters, the hereditary mishaps of the past were corrected and the masculine supremacy ordained, apparently, by God, reinstated. When three more daughters arrived after the son, the existential threat still hovered. But, as my father was always telling us, 'it takes a lot to extinguish life' and an only son is still a son. With my father injecting new life into the Towneley name and Only Brother safely delivered, the restoration part of the job was done. Now, and with some relief, 'no more slippage' established itself as the main purpose of my father's life.

One change that wasn't slippage in my father's opinion was the creation of a garden. It was the kind of garden his grandmother would have loved had the industrial smoke, open-cast coaling, war and weather not restricted her to a straggle of hardy survivors. The end of the war, the decline of open-cast coaling and the looming Clean Air Act would mean that everybody could breathe more easily, plants included. A new garden, designed by Jim Russell, garden-designer to grandees, would be the precise opposite of slippage.

The garden design was ambitious: two beds fifty yards long and ten yards wide separated by forty yards of lawn; the planting elaborate; the vision bold. Almost a thousand feet above sea-level, any kind of garden, let alone a grand one, would still be weather-battered, so ambition, planting and vision would be protected by assuming from the adjacent field the few acres needed to cultivate a shelterbelt of trees. To do this my father had to consult Mr. M., his land-agent.

Mr. M. had been my great-grandmother's land-agent. More than that. He was her mentor. It was he who inducted her into her role as doyenne of these unpromising acres, a role which, even as the daughter of the senior Towneley co-heiress, had formed no part of her girlish hopes or expectations. He was her guide as she swapped hunting with the Rothschilds at Chantilly and the high culture and amusements of European sophistication for breeding Ayrshire cows and Lonks sheep in a bog. He was the guru who had successfully guided the ingenue. But the guru wasn't a fan of the shelterbelt. Not a fan at all.

It wasn't kindness that prevented my father riding roughshod and simply ordering in the planters. By his own admission it was cowardice. Overruling Mr. M. would be a first. His grandmother had never done it. A first overruling risked slippage of the most dangerous kind. The shelterbelt might be fundamental to the garden's survival but the slippery slope menaced. 'I funked it,' he said.

'Funked it?' This was 2007, and at my father's dictation I was typing a piece on the garden solicited by a magazine. 'Funked' wasn't a word I'd ever heard my father use. It didn't seem his kind of word. He could see my fingers suspended over the keys. 'Funked,' he said. 'Write it down. I funked it.' There was a moment when he could, I think, have cried – that shelterbelt! that shelterbelt! In the end he began to laugh – crying over a shelterbelt! So I began to laugh. Quite unexpectedly we were in one of those warm moments that arise as if from nowhere and which remain warm in the memory, rising again at odd times, again for no apparent reason. Sometimes they make you cry, not from sadness or even missing the person, just crying, I suppose, for the unrepeatableness of a spontaneous connection. The funk and the shelterbelt went into the magazine. I never heard my father use the word again.

Not that 'funking' was over. Nor was it limited to the shelterbelt. 'Whose estate is it?' my mother fumed when some years later my father was still simply agreeing, unquestioning, to anything Mr. M, and later his son, another Mr. M., suggested. When these suggestions included sales of farms, something my mother felt was akin to sacrilege, she was incandescent. If my father needed money, why couldn't he earn it like everybody else?

Here my father was on firm, unfunking ground. Sales suggested by Mr. M. or even Mr. M.'s son, could never be slippage. How could they be? Mr. M. had been his grandmother's bible. Anything suggested by him was irreproachable, undebateable, unimpeachable. As for earning money, even *thinking* about money was slippage beyond slippage. 'You have a No. 1 household account and a No. 2 household account,' he told my mother. It was as near to money-talk as he ever got, his panic at coming even that close apparent in his expression, alarmed as a judge bested by the accused.

'But what's each account supposed to cover?' my mother wailed, waving the two chequebooks in the air like flags of surrender. 'How much is in them? What happens if there's nothing in them?' These were rhetorical questions. She knew and my father knew and everybody knew that neither he nor anybody else knew the answers. My father himself kept wads of cash in his diary. That was what diaries were for. According to my father, pocket-money for children was ridiculous. As for allowances when we grew older, these would be set at £25 per quarter, the same as his grandmother's allowance in the later 1800s. What was good enough for her, etc. etc. How other money worked in the Not-So-Grand house remained as mysterious as the Holy Trinity.

I'd like to slip in here that slippage wasn't always as expected. In 1969 or 1970, in London for the dentist – my father didn't believe there were dentists in Burnley, and himself also went to London to have his hair cut – he announced that I, Second Sister and Oldest Sister, aged roughly twelve, thirteen and fourteen, would visit the newish Way In on the fourth floor of Harrods. Mingling with the hip-people wasn't slippage. Choosing anything we liked wasn't slippage. It would be slippage only if we stayed inside the shop, or any shop, for more than ten minutes. I don't recall what Oldest Sister and Second Sister grabbed. In fewer than five minutes my arms were full of a green velvet trouser suit, a cascading shirt, a pair of long shiny pull-up boots and bright shiny things that were just bright shiny things. We tried nothing on. My father paid without demur. Roughly nine minutes later we were back on the pavement, everybody happy if a little confused, and definitely no slippage at all.

The garden survived without its shelterbelt. As for any danger posed by children's games, this was easily countered. We were set loose in the small wood that dropped away from the house beyond the high wall of the bottom lawn and towards the railway field. In spring, bluebells carpeted either side of a nobbly path, and the sunken remains of some kind of dwelling offered intrepid child explorers hiding places prickly with fallen beechnuts and sycamore spinners.

This part of the garden wasn't ours and I never thought of it as our father's. It was just the garden. Enhanced by Jim Russell's planting suggestions but deliberately not controlled, this Secret Garden, as it was soon christened, was the obvious place for the swing and the sandpit. Here, children could neither be seen nor heard by grown-ups. Even better, grown-ups could neither be seen nor heard by children. Best of all, beneath the bluebells, beneath untold millennia of fallen leaves, beneath anything my father, Jim Russell or anybody could impose, were the wonders of ants and earwigs, of old stone and old bones. Here were glass bottles, some with plugs intact, others open and sticky with the lees of substances once important to somebody. With absolutely no danger of slippage at all, these wonders were ours.

5

MORE THAN USUAL PERVERSITY

OUR FAITH – I always think of it as faith, never as 'religion' – wasn't a frowning creature. It didn't loom over us like a censorious black cloud, discharging disapproval like hailstones. Certainly, it had its 'loomy' moments – Catholic guilt seeps in early and embeds like the nag of tinnitus. No fire and brimstone though. It was just that more than any past Towneley distinctions, we were brought up to remember that we were the religious heirs not just of our recusant family, but also of those men and occasional women whose lives were prised from them in the grisly ways popular during the Reformation. If Catholicism was our duty, recusancy set our standard. Lord Burghley, chief adviser to Elizabeth I and a scourge of Catholics, could never have guessed how proud he would make my father by labelling us, clinging to our faith, a family of 'unusual perversity'.

Here we are, then, being 'unusually perverse' on, say, 27th February 1966. To most people, 27th February 1966 is simply the third Sunday in February. Thoughts turn to spring and possibly the world cup in July. To most Catholics it's the first Sunday of Lent. In the chilly parish church the priest urges fasting and discomforts. To us in the Not-So-Grand house 27 February 1966 is Quadragesima.

As happens every Sunday, my father has pushed round the sofas, arranged the armchairs and finally drawn back the heavy silk curtain that, to the surprise and occasional alarm of guests, hides the smallest oratory in Britain. With an altar fashioned by workmen on the estate, a stained-glass window created by our cousin Patrick Reyntiens and two long thin religious paintings of medieval hues, this little space is bigger than spring, bigger than the world cup, bigger than anything the parish priest can urge. This oratory is the deep heart of the Not-So-Grand house. It signifies the ultimate 'no more slippage'. Ironic, then, that it's tagged onto the end of a new drawing room, the bottom part of an extension finished just in time for the birth of Only Brother in 1962 and, my parents hoped, vainly as it turned out, in time for many more brothers to come.

Oratory notwithstanding, you may well ask how the extension squared with domestic 'no more slippage'. After all, nobody extends a house whose essentials don't work without fixing the essentials. My father hit on the perfect solution. Instead of employing a domestic architect he employed George Pace, a church architect, with the result that far from the new bit of the house infecting the old, the old bit infected the new. More taps that seldom ran. More loos with arbitrary flushing. Perhaps at the tearful request of our frozen mother, one concession only was made. The drawing room was to have underfloor heating. My father countered this by so rarely turning it on that, like the Assumption, it remained an article of faith.

So, here we are in the ironic new drawing room, oratory curtain drawn back. From his big wooden cross Jesus is gazing down on a pleasingly medieval mise en scène: my mother and father on prie-dieus at the front, my mother's mantilla all drapey, my father's face frowny with prayer or perhaps he just wants breakfast – in the Not-So-Grand house pre-Mass fasting is still severe. Behind our parents and carefully dressed by Nanny in matching dresses or kilts with bodices, we three oldest daughters aged nine, eight and seven are sitting in a prim line on the sofa, ready to stand or kneel as Mass requires. And that's all we have to do: sit, stand, kneel. As girls we play no part in the actual Mass because as girls we are nothing. Worse than nothing. We are contaminants. We can't touch anything, not the vestments, not any of the altar furniture, not the vessel carrying the water in which the priest washes his hands. Any active participation is reserved for real people, i.e. men. This doesn't strike us as odd. It's how things are. Any change would obviously be serious slippage.

Oh, I almost forgot. On Quadragesima, as on other Sundays, before Mass we must go to my father's library, kneel on the rug in front of the library fire and confess our sins. Our confessor is the Jesuit priest who has come over from Stonyhurst, the Catholic boys school roughly fifteen miles away. He sits in judgement. This wouldn't be so bad if my father's portrait wasn't glowering down like God the Father from above the fire, or if the priest was anonymous. But there is my painted father, and there is the flesh-and-blood priest with whom, once we graduate from the nursery to the dining room, we have breakfast, with whom we go for walks, who says Midnight Mass at Christmas and on whose bed, along with every other person in the house on Christmas Eve, Father Christmas deposits a stocking. While we will eventually know ordinary things about him – how he likes his eggs boiled, how he butters his toast, whether he takes sugar in his tea – he already knows the worst things about us.

I suppose we could have addressed this uncomfortable imbalance by insisting on only confessing to the unfamiliar parish priest in the parish church in Burnley. But even that wasn't safe. Unless we adopted Lancashire accents we betrayed our identity the moment we opened our mouths and said in accents like the Queen's 'Bless me, Father, for I have sinned'. Another option was to follow our father's example and confess only abroad, to priests you guessed spoke no English. That seemed pleasingly radical. Also unpleasingly risky. We might not go abroad. If we did, we might forget and unwittingly choose a third option: not confessing at all. This would probably send you to hell. What to do for the best?

I confess now that as a child mostly I repeated the sin list my whole primary school class compiled with the help of the nuns: 'I have been disobedient, told lies, been unkind. Please, Father, that is all I can remember'. Some weeks none of these things were true so my confession was itself a lie. With the strange logic of religion, this lie made it true. I had, though, nearly always sinned by omission or by thinking the wrong thing. Kneeling before the priest in the library, I couldn't list these sins. They weren't awful. That was the trouble. Awful had a certain glamour. My sins were disappointingly pedestrian. Like everybody else I resented being told to eat mashed turnip because 'people in the world are starving'. Perhaps not like everybody else, I wasn't thrilled when my mother told me she was having another baby, although my mother not being thrilled herself might have added interesting complexities. In any event, what I said or didn't say didn't seem to matter. For a penance, I was always given three Hail Marys with the occasional Our Father lobbed in for, I assume, variety. In teenagerdom I was tempted to fabricate outrageous sins, spill out a murder, perhaps, or say the word 'boy'. It wouldn't have worked. Father would have been gently understanding of a murder and since my boy vocabulary was limited to 'boy', he would have seen through that at once. It was back to the old list. If Father was bored, under the Seal of Confession he was obliged to keep that to himself.

Just as a courtroom never quite shakes off its glower, so the library never shook off its confessional edge. In an article on the Roxburghe Club which described my father's library as 'small but spell-binding', I thought how a visitor to a library sees only the custodian's public taste. However 'spell-binding' the rarities, the complete collections and the intricate bindings, these are in many ways far less interesting than what the visitor can never hear: the conversations and the silences; the thoughts thought and the thoughts abandoned; the secrets shared and the secrets withheld. And, in our case, the confessions. However boring to oneself, confessions are always fascinating to others. So it was that in common with many libraries, the library in the Not-So-Grand house was more than the sum of its treasures. As confessees we might, I suppose, have grown to hate it. But though our sins remain hanging in the air, the library still feels a place of safety. As a Catholic, when you confess, however dull your sins, you're absolved. There's a kind of safety in that.

Enough of confession. Here we are, back at Quadragesima 1966. Some Smaller Sisters are yet to be born. I can't remember where Only Brother sat. I see quite clearly Oldest Sister, Second Sister and myself. I know that instead of focusing on God I'm mesmerised by two sins that I haven't confessed, and a possibility so frightening I have to squeeze my hands together. The first sin relates to the bodice of my kilt. I hate that bodice. It's sleeveless, white, with buttons down the front and buttons attaching it to the kilt. The buttons are bumpy. The armholes are in the wrong place. It makes me look fat. I wear it with hate in my heart. Hate is a sin. The second sin relates to Oldest Sister's fainting spells, against which she is allowed a glass of hot Ribena before Mass whilst the rest of us are allowed nothing. Why has God reserved fainting for her? I'm envious. Envy is a sin. Then there is the fearful thing which comes at the end of Mass and which is still a fearful thing so I'll work up to it.

At 08.30 sharp my father, who acts as altar server, rings a silver bell and we stand as Father T. –always Father T. until it was Father M. – processes from the hall, past the gents loo, down the steps and through the carved double doors that came from the Brussels house of Great-Aunt Adrienne. All I know of Great-Aunt Adrienne is that to Granny's disgust, during the war she continued life exactly as if the war wasn't happening. On Quadragesima Father T. wears the purple vestments my father has laid out for him on the special flat tray in the hall. The vestments, commissioned by my great-grandmother, are silk, embroidered by hand. My favourites are the rose vestments and 'best white'. Crowning them all is the gold Whalley chasuble, not commissioned by Great Granny. Stitched in the mid-15th century and saved from Reformation destruction by John Towneley, it's thick enough to deflect a bullet.

February is cold. Logs blaze in the big fireplace, its pale stone surround carved with the four crests united in my parents' marriage:

the Towneley sparrowhawk, the Koch de Gooreynd dove, the Fitzherbert fist and the Scrope chough. A shuffle, a cough, and Mass begins
as it has begun since time immemorial, '*In nomine Patris et Filii et
Spiritus Sancti*' . . .

Given my father's unwavering commitment to 'backwards', or
at least standing still, it's as ironic as the new drawing room that
the central Catholic event of our childhoods, the Second Vatican
Council (1962-65), exhorts us to leap forward. We're to cast off the
'betrayal and ruination' old-order narratives and embrace the new
order of 'human relationships'. Slippage? This is an avalanche. Out
will go the 'blessed mutter of the Mass'[*]; in with the vernacular. Out
with plainchant; in with guitars. Out with Faith of My Fathers; in
with Kum Bah Yah. And horror of horrors, women will be allowed
to creep nearer the altar than the sacristy mop cupboard or, in our
case, the second row sofa.

My father doesn't panic. Here in our drawing room church he
steadfastly ignores the exhortations of the pope. Mass remains in
Latin. No guitar twangs. Girls remain contaminants. People might
judge it intransigence, resistance even. In truth it's not even 'more
than usual perversity'. It's simply that my father believes, and through
him we believe, that Towneleys are more Catholic than any Vatican
Council. Towneleys are more Catholic than the pope. Towneleys
are indeed more Catholic than God.

Thus I learn early that obedience isn't absolute. We must obey
Nanny, our parents, all nuns and priests. But in any contest between
obedience and the slippery slope, the slippery slope always wins. This
seems entirely right and proper. Anyway, who is going to check that
we're complying with the new order? Not Father T., who wouldn't
want to jeopardise his bibulous weekends at the Not-So-Grand
house. Not the parish priest since we never see him. Obviously not
the pope, who seems unlikely to visit. That leaves only God, and

*   Browning, R. 'The Bishop Orders His Tomb at Saint Praxted's Church'

against recusant Catholics He has very little leverage. So on we go through the Confiteor beating our breasts, through the Epistle, the Gospel, the Credo, the offertory, the consecration and communion in the unslippaged way our ancestors did before us. It's after the final blessing and dismissal that the hand-squeezing moment arrives. It's nothing to do with slippage or ancestors.

Before processing out, my father hands Father T. a laminated A4-sized card on which is printed the Prayer for the Queen, surprisingly, perhaps, Elizabeth II, our earthly queen, not Mary, Queen of Heaven. 'We are loyal to both pope and crown,' my father often states, as though Lord Burghley had turned up for an interrogation.

'O Lord save Elizabeth our queen,' intones Father T.

Mass being officially over, we girls can now respond. 'And hear us on the day we call upon Thee,' we chorus.

'Almighty God,' continues Father T, 'we pray for Thy servant Elizabeth, our queen, now by Thy mercy reigning over us, adorn her more with every virtue, remove all evil from her path' –

Now my hands are squashed together so hard they've turned white. If the priest's next words are 'and vanquish her enemies' we're all doomed. Only to be said 'in time of war', those words will signal that Russia has dropped the bomb. By the end of Mass, the Not-So-Grand house and everybody in it, which is pretty much everybody and everything I love in the world, will be obliterated, with the terrible, conflicting possibility of me being the only survivor. Every Sunday, every Holiday of Obligation, in other words every time we hear Mass, our fate rests on this A4 laminated card. And the prayer for the queen coming at the end of Mass, the threat hovers throughout, even at magical Midnight Mass at Christmas.

I'm twenty-four before I actually hear the words 'and vanquish her enemies' and to me they're far more ominous than pictures of the taskforce sent to retake the Falkland Islands. I hear the words again in 2003 during the Iraq war. My knuckles are still clenched. These days they're clenched pretty much all the time.

In case you were wondering: we weren't entirely unquestioning of our steadfast antiquated Catholicism. Notwithstanding the all-en-compassing slippery slope, the 'steadfast' narrative did raise some obvious niggles. The Dukes of Norfolk, for example, our relations through various marriages, some long ago, some not so long ago, were also Catholics, so how come they hadn't sunk into a Not-So-Grand house? Indeed, their castle, fortune and prestige survived not only intact but flourishing. Same with the Camoys at enchanted Stonor. So apart from the glamour of ancestral blood-shedding and suffering, exactly where had all that pain and perversity got us Towneleys? Mass in the drawing room and a 15th century bullet-proof chasuble didn't seem quite enough in worldly terms. Since no Towneley was officially a martyr, not quite enough in heavenly terms either.

Then there was The Big Lie. Never mentioned was the fact that our Great-x-3 aunt, Lady O'Hagan, she who naughtily ground her cheroots stubs into the wooden floor and then sold our Grand House to the Burnley Council, hadn't bought into the 'steadfast' narrative at all. Without even a threat of torture she'd 'lapsed' - Catholics use that word with special disdain - into Unitarianism.

It's roughly 1974 before I'm brave enough to raise Alice O'Hagan with my father. I'm looking at him from the other side of the library fire. I'm 16. He's 53. Dressed as always by his London tailor, with a pink woollen tie - 'ties are so warm!' - and the startlingly bright socks in which he delighted, he's sitting deep in his dilapidated armchair. Perched on his knee is a biography of some long dead or just dead politico, or what we now call a 'creative', a term he would have scorned as vainglorious. A log basket in the library would be slippage so every so often he makes the trek into the passage and through to the hall to collect a log from the logbox by the front door. His movements are brisk, his whole short body - we're not a tall family - tilting purposefully forward. If he's irritated, which he often is either by something in his book, or a thought, or us, or having to get up for the logs - non-slippage and suffering some-times go together - he shakes his hands, one at each side, like a dog shaking off water. In other ways the dog image is wrong. My father isn't remotely animal. He's more a figure in a nineteenth century painting – Sir Irritated Steadfast of Non-Slippage. Something like that. Balanced on the springs poking through my chair, a chair that, you've guessed it, has 'always been there', and fuelled by a sudden rush of rebellion, I want Sir Irritated Steadfast to slip.

'We never talk about Alice O'Hagan,' I say boldly.

'Nothing to say.'

'There's lots to say! She rode a bicycle and smoked cheroots. She presided over the Clog Fund!'

'She died before I was born.'

'Only a month. Did she and Great Granny [aunt and niece] like each other? Did they ever meet? Did they discuss their faith?'

He narrows his eyes. 'I've no idea.'

'Did you never ask Great Granny?'

'Why should I?'

'Well,' I'm faltering in the face of the barbed brick wall. 'It's always nice to know things.'

'I can't think of any use for that.' He waits, the kind of waiting sharpened on your discomfort like a knife on a whetstone.

I can't quite give up. 'Great Granny might have known why Alice O'Hagan stopped being a Catholic. I mean,' I say rather desperately, 'perhaps she thought that those who suffered suffered a long time ago so . . .'

'So?'

'Well, so much time had passed . . .'

'Time? What's time got to do with it?' My father snorts with the particular contempt he reserves for cowards who, as he sees it, benefit spiritually from the bravery of others. 'And what do you know about suffering?'

You can't talk about suffering with somebody who fought in the war. 'Nothing.'

He returns to his book, an easy victory. I return to my book, an inevitable defeat.

Later, I rehearse with my dog the conversation as it should have gone but was never going to. Momentarily I envy people unencumbered, as I see it, by 'no more slippage'. But at sixteen I'm also beginning to appreciate that 'no more slippage' is the bulwark on which the Not-So-Grand house leans. Without it, we're just another family on the slide. Looking at my father across the library fire the following evening I sense he's waiting for more questions. I come from a family of unusual perversity so I say nothing. We read.

Suddenly he says, 'Do you feel like a glass of champagne?' It's not an olive branch. He just knows that I like champagne. He likes it too.

'I do,' I say, and once it's poured into the silver mug given to his grandfather by his godfather the Duke of Wellington, we don't return to our books. We don't talk about anything in particular. We're just there, at home, and with no perversity at all, it's enough.

6

SOUNDS AND SIGHTS

CHAMPAGNE GLASSES WERE regularly filled in the library by my father. With similar regularity, the coal hods were filled in the coal shed by Robert, earning pocket-money in his final years at school. Sturdy creatures, the hods, cylindrical, once silvery now blackened, with two handles one above the other. You could muster a good swing before digging into the coal with the tongue. 'Tongue' suggests a glide like a duckbilled platypus into mud. There was no gliding. Robert had to jigger the hod about to capture the lumps, all different in size and shape. The scrape was the sound of capture and escape, the evading lumps toppling noisily down the great coal pile to lodge at Robert's feet. When the hod was yanked upright and the coal tumbled to the bottom, the sound changed from scrape jigger to the cascading rumble of an angry God clearing his throat. Then there would be a small pause as Robert bent down to toss the errant hunks back up the pile for capture another day. A dull clang signalled the full hod being swung to one side and dumped into the line of hods awaiting transport into the house. Full hods sat in the scullery like a row of fat nuns queueing for confession.

Hod filling happened roughly four times a week, the coal destined for the old Aga, the nursery stove or my mother's bedroom fire. Although my parents always slept together, my father viewed any acknowledgement of this as suspiciously slippery slope. Their room was always known as my mother's room and the fire as my mother's fire.

The old Aga was a cream-coloured four-oven sulky Methuselah that squatted in the kitchen like an ancient relation of anchorous bulk. Nobody knew its exact age. It had simply 'always been there', a palpable untruth nobody ever disputed. In the middle of the hotplate underneath the lefthand lid was a small round mini-plate with two grooves for the pronged extractor grip. Plate out and suddenly, thrillingly, you could feel the pulsing glow, the heat surging upwards thick and hot like the breath of an animal pent up beyond endurance. Quick quick, heave the hod, balance it over the hole and tip it over, black meat to red heart. Still not without resistance though. Robert had to shake the hod – shruh clatter, shruh clatter, shruh clatter – to get all the coal into the Aga's maw. When the first hod was empty, quick quick with the second, the glow blanketed by the new coal but always gathering strength to break through. Two hods, and then Robert swept escaped fragments and coal dust into the hole with the soft brush kept on the back of the Aga. Slot the plate back into the hole. Close the Aga lid. Now the beast was fed, Robert wiped his nose and gathered up the hods, clanging them together as he carried them back into the scullery to their allotted place in the empty hod line. Then he walked home.

I don't know what Robert thought of us, the beneficiaries of hod-filling who never filled a hod ourselves. Like us, he may have accepted that this was the natural order of things, seduced by the fact that whilst the house was Not-So-Grand, the mood music was very grand indeed, so the lives of hod-fillers and hod-beneficiaries ran on parallel lines. Maybe as he filled the hods he was already planning his future departure for the richer, sunnier living which, through his own graft and imagination, he soon realised in South Africa. Perhaps he simply counted the empties in and the full hods out. If we met now, would those ancient hierarchies still persist even if we pretended they didn't? Class boundaries may be more smudged these days but ingrained as coaldust, they never quite disappear.

Like the Aga, the nursery stove was filled straight from the hod.

In my mother's bedroom the coal arrived in the grate by hand from a brass coal-scuttle which itself was filled from a white enamel bucket which in turn had been filled from the hod which had been filled by Robert. After all this filling, the fire still needed coaxing not to puff smoke like a mill chimney. To this end it ate spills, thick screws of newspaper twisted into knots with two tails by Mrs N., the mother of Robert.

Mrs N. was small and round, with two strong legs, no middle to speak of and the cleaning energy of a dervish. She embraced every job, from washing the delicate china to scrubbing the outside loo – 'must mek it nice for Mr. H.' (the gardener) – with the zeal of a true enthusiast. She made the spills as she sat at the kitchen table having a brew, her legs swinging, chirruping unrecognisable songs in a high reedy voice of very particular sweetness. Mrs N. loved the Not-So-Grand house. She loved us. She loved to chat. She didn't hold with working hours, as in hours of work you counted and for which you were paid. To Mrs N., work was life, and life was up to you. She was frightened of only two things: dying owing even one penny, and the hoover.

Maud N. – always Mrs N. to us – had been married to Alf, a farm worker. We knew how much she respected him because 'the only time we used the front door was to get Alf out in 'is coffin'. When it rained, her house flooded and Mrs N. was often seen scurrying across the field to jam in the board which prevented her belongings floating away. She never complained. She did, though, have opinions. What he calls 'going to work', she would say of people in what we now call bullshit jobs. Mrs N. would never have used that phrase herself. In all the vicissitudes of her life, and there were many, I never heard her swear.

Every Sunday, Mrs N. walked the three miles to see her mother. Even had there been a bus, she wouldn't have used it. She didn't want people to know her business. And she had a lot of business, her many children producing many grandchildren and, more quickly than perhaps anticipated, grandchildren producing great-grandchildren.

Mrs N. was no starry-eyed matriarch. Her family could do right and they could do wrong, but they were her family and her loyalty to them was as rock solid as it was to us.

Along with fluorescent soft toys and knitting for the Sea Cadets, Mrs N. liked picturesque calendars, but actual time was marked in hair dye. There wasn't a colour she hadn't tried with greater or lesser success. When her eyes began to fail and the colours turned out not quite as she imagined, she remained as undaunted as when she discovered she'd been using oven-spray for hairspray. 'No real harm done.'

Harm was a relative concept. When those same eyes told her that the Not-So-Grand house kitchen needed redecorating, my parents being abroad and the house empty of children, she rolled up her sleeves. Paint was procured – matt, gloss, what was the difference if all white or whiteish. She stood on tiptoe on the kitchen table to start on the ceiling. Not much paint clung to the ceiling but a remarkable amount clung to the light fittings, to the table itself and to the Aga. Two pictures hung on the kitchen wall, one of Towneley's prize-winning Royal Butterfly (confusingly, a bull), the other of Fidelity, one of his wives. The paint splatters now decorating Butterfly and Fidelity puzzled Mrs N. The pictures were miles from the ceiling. No matter! There was nothing she couldn't clean. Thus, with cloth, turpentine and every good intention, Mrs N. snipped thousands from the value of these originals. It didn't help that during a vigorous bout of rubbing Fidelity sliced through Butterfly's canvas. Sensing things were more amiss than she thought, Mrs N. taped up the gashes and repainted the smudgy bits with the ceiling paint. 'I've cleaned yer pictures,' she said to my father on his return. When he didn't immediately respond, she added cheerfully, waving an empty gallon drum of sodium hypochlorite, 'I've cleaned yer bath as well'.

The Not-So-Grand house was unimaginable without Mrs N. We never truly had to since once she 'retired' in the mid 1980s and moved to a dwelling less flood-prone she often returned. 'I've been moidering about them backdoor flags,' she'd say. 'I'll just come and give them a good doin'.' Only death stopped her.

Somewhere I have a photograph of Mrs N. in the garden, perched in a deckchair like a plump contented wren. I don't need the photograph to see her. She's as embedded in my heart's eye as the scrape of the coalhods in my heart's ear.

7

MYSTERIOUS VAGARIES

I WANT TO go back a little because, as I write, a puzzle keeps bubbling up. In part, I think the bubbling is caused by my reaching the age at which my mother died. From now on, I'll be older than she ever was. Though it's not unusual, it can be a bit of a mind-twister. My mother died in 2001. She was 65, which seemed oldish then and now seems frighteningly young. If you've not yet overtaken, or never overtake, your mother, you'll miss the sudden clutches of astonishment that grip when least expected. Older than one's mother! So you're not missing out on much except, perhaps, if your own clock does wind past your mother's, the special poignancy of puzzles rendered insoluble by death. My puzzle is the puzzle of my parents' marriage.

A little context. My father's paternal grandmother and my mother's maternal grandmother being sisters, my parents had known of each other from childhood. Their first real meeting, though, was through my mother's pony, Gypsy, whom my father was sent to collect from the railway station – my mother took her pony to what was euphemistically called 'school' since, according to Ma, it didn't involve lessons. My father hated ponies, my mother adored them. Nonetheless, my father suffered, if that's the right word, a coup de foudre – love at first sight. His love had its oddities even then. In a letter shortly after he'd proposed and been accepted he wrote 'I should care only mildly if we ended up together in a debtors' prison surrounded by dotty children in a beggars' opera'. How mild is mild? How dotty is dotty? How beggarish is beggary? My mother wasn't bothered by these uncertainties. Scandalously for Catholics of the time, my father's parents had divorced and my mother believed divorce, like chicken-pox, was catching. My father must have reassured her. They married in London in 1955 at St. James's, Spanish Place. She was 20, he 34.

A photograph captures her in demure figure-hugging lace, a string of pearls round her neck, and him, slim, shoes shining, morning coat buttoned, holding her hand tightly. She looks older than 20, he younger than 34. I'm still struck by my father's displayed ear, his hair cut neatly that morning probably at Trumper's, the London barber. Though age did its usual work on the rest of him, even in his coffin aged nearly 101 my father's ear remained unchanged. I sometimes imagine all the things it had heard: the bells of Oxford; the plaintive bugles, in vain recalling his platoon over the swollen River Garigliano during the war; the brass band outside the Not-So-Grand house welcoming him and my mother back from honeymoon. Then all the things that went in but remained unheard, unhearing being another useful bulwark against slippage. Pregnant and lonely, always cold and unable to manage the Not-So-Grand house servants, my mother asked if they could spend their first married Christmas with her parents. Deaf to my mother's misery, my father refused. 'My grandmother never went away for Christmas so here we'll stay.' After my mother's death he remembered this refusal. Such hauntings were only occasional. He wasn't a man given to regrets.

The English side of my father's family, the Berties, were grand; the Belgian, the Koch de Gooreynds, rich. My mother's family were ancient Scropes and ancient Fitzherberts so my parents' match was made in Catholic heaven. Nonetheless – and here's the nub of the puzzle – it's with only minor disrespect to my father that I ask 'why did she do it?' She, the lively, adored middle-daughter of loving parents; he, the irritable, impatient, uncomfortable older son of a chilly mother and an absent boulevardier father.

My mother – unschooled, instinctive, empathetic, imaginative. My father – urbane yet donnish, of strict and unbending habits, sentimental but with an empathy bypass. My father's preferred life was books, concerts, restaurants. When I imagine him, he's indoors and sedentary. My mother, though she did love music and beautiful things, was a do-er and maker. In a restaurant, her main interest was the kitchen, and she was less interested in the cooking than in helping mop the floors. When I imagine her, she's outside on a horse. Yet there they were, soldered together by the unbreakable bond of Catholic marriage and the mysterious vagaries of love.

And the vagaries were mysterious since, as you already know, any reference to love except in a letter had my father shying away like a cartoon character from a cliff-edge. Love, like grace, should be so discreet as to be invisible. Luckily, my mother didn't need to talk about love. She carried it with her. This wasn't because she was soft. Had she been soft she'd never have survived. It was because my mother had an integrity, a truthfulness about her that shone from within. When people spoke to her or of her, their faces softened, their eyes lit up. 'I allus think on yer mother when I'm shavin',' old Lord Rhodes, mill-owner, politician and one of the bravest men I ever met, once told me. 'Best start to m'day.'

Having early on had any potential love for, or even interest in, the Not-So-Grand house stamped out by 'if it was good enough for my grandmother etc.' my mother soon stopped looking inside the house. Instead, she looked out of the windows. In 1955 what she saw was hardly encouraging. With the Clean Air Act a year away and taking further years to take effect, no birds sang. Glancing one way she was presented with the remains of the open-cast coaling and glancing the other, the chimneys of Burnley. Pendle glowered beyond. Nobody wise took advantage of the rare sunshine to hang out their laundry since once gathered back in every item was grey and gritty, as if Burnley had coughed and used the washing as a handkerchief. Nonetheless, possibly because she didn't take in the washing herself, something caught her. Perhaps it was the implacability, the take-it-or-piss-off-ness of it. Perhaps it was the draw of the hills, their changing colours, their openness. Maybe that was the start, with the deeper love blossoming quite a bit later, perhaps after 1960 when, before the Not-So-Grand house's extension was built, there was a flirtation with moving. The flirtation was brief. Moving being more slippery slope than extending, along came George Pace, in came the diggers and up went the scaffolding. With divorce utterly unthinkable, my mother knew then that she was stuck in the Not-So-Grand house, on this hill, with these views, for the rest of her life. Such certainty would have killed some people. It breathed some of that Burnley grit into my mother. She'd have a horse. She'd ride the moors. She'd hunt. Despite the house, despite all these bloody babies, despite my father, eventually eventually eventually she'd live a life that was hers.

My mother was no martyr. She simply embodied the stubborn patience of a landscape waiting for better weather that will, in time, arrive. I think this stubborn patience, which is a kind of love, saw her through those first bleak years of marriage. And it wasn't all bleak. I can still hear her reading to us – *At the Back of the North Wind*, *The Princess and the Goblin*, *Black Beauty* – completely absorbed in the story, pointing out little details in the pictures as though discovering them for herself for the first time. She had infectious zest, unsurprising as she wasn't that much older than us. I remember her 29th birthday quite clearly. Our mother is now old, I thought as Nanny brushed my hair. I was frightened. Old people died. Nanny finished brushing and turned me round to inspect her work. I looked at Nanny. She was old, far older than my mother, and she wasn't dead. Maybe I could put off worrying until my mother was 30.

Married now for forty years myself, I feel I should understand better my parents' marriage. I do understand my mother's horror of divorce. She'd seen what fractures it caused in my father's family. I think I understand why, as she lay dying, my mother wanted my father, and my father alone, with her. Quite apart from dying being an intimate undertaking and seven children constituting too big an audience, my mother was gifting my father a final reassurance. Whatever the vicissitudes of her life, whatever the early miseries, the divergences, the conflicts, the mutual infuriations, they were still, in all the deep respects that matter, that couple holding hands in the wedding photograph.

I'm tempted to say that in the final analysis aren't we all the couples in our wedding photographs. But when I look at my own wedding photographs that's not what I see. Though I was twenty-six to my mother's twenty and my experience of life far broader, my wedding photographs reveal a bride and groom yet to settle into themselves and each other. My mother, despite her youth, appears already to have settled into herself, and though the future is always uncertain, to be stepping into it confident in the choice she's made. My father appears less at ease, more as if the ceremony and photographs are something to get through before married life can start. In none of their wedding photographs are my parents looking at each other. In none of them truly smiling. Yet there's a kind of togetherness in the way they're facing the press photographers who always throng to a 'society' wedding. This togetherness isn't the cliché 'us against them'. It's more 'this is us, full stop'. That's what I mean by 'the deep respects that matter' – that they started out 'this is us, full stop' and that's how they remained.

One strange thing. It strikes me quite forcibly that despite 'this is us, full stop' I can't remember any conversations between my mother and father alone, with us children as onlookers. No conversations in the car between them in the front, and us listening in the back. No conversations over dinner during which we children were silent. No desultory chats in the library whilst we read our books. I can recall certain exchanges: my father barking at my mother to hurry up or they'd be late for some official do and my mother calling 'I'm on my way down' (which meant she was still washing her hair). I can hear my father stamping about in the hall, muttering, and my mother's plaintive 'we're in plenty of time'. I can hear a small altercation as my mother tries to jam into a small smart bag all the rubbish from the tatty sack into which so much was bundled and so little could ever be found. 'Come ON, Mary.' 'I'm coming, I'm coming.' Exchanges are not conversations.

Yet now I come to think of it, what exclusively parental conversations will my own children remember? Don't most parents save those conversations for when the children have departed? Not that the conversations are secret. Usually they're rather dull. It's more that parents have lives together, and they have lives with their children. Perhaps in this one respect if in few others my parents were perfectly ordinary.

But even if my mother knew her own mind; even if she felt she was ready; even if my father, so much older and more sophisticated, seemed an enticing prospect, I can't quite put the question 'why did she do it?' to bed. Maybe she'd be as unable to answer the question as I am. She'd probably wonder why I felt it mattered. 'Mysterious vagaries,' she'd say. 'When you get married, aren't they all you need?'

8

THROWING THE CAT

IT SOUNDS POMPOUSLY grand to say we had quite a few nannies so I'd like to be clear: we didn't have them all at once – a nanny each, as it were. Anyway, properly grand families had one nanny, inherited from ages past, her own surname wiped out and forgotten perhaps even by her (always a her) as without (visible) demur she adopted the surname of her charges. We had friends with nannies like that. Our nannies kept their own names. One did lose her sanity; that wasn't the same thing at all.

Over nannies, Evelyn Waugh and P. L. Travers have a lot to answer for. Real nannies, and by 'real' I mean fixture-and-fitting nannies who arrived and stayed sometimes for decades; nannies who darned but didn't drive; nannies who turned collars but didn't cook; and however long they stayed never sat comfortably in the drawing room or signed the visitors book – these nannies were neither Nanny Hawkins nor Mary Poppins. It's true that our Nanny D. was gentle and our Nanny E. spit-spot. Any resemblance stops there.

In the 1960s, nannies were substantial, authoritative, the nursery their sovereign territory. Unlike capricious Poppins, and even more unlike modern nannies, most old-world nannies hadn't chosen nannydom. Many were pushed into it as a job that required no education, brought in a small salary and offered a way of life at least potentially more physically comfortable than the homes in which they had grown up. At interview in those days nannies were never asked if they liked children. Lucky, as many didn't. Not that that would have counted against them for my father. He didn't like children either. My mother might have thought liking children of some importance had liking not been trumped by simply finding a nanny who'd agree to live in a soot-stained, scantily-plumbed, chilly Not-So-Grand house in north-east Lancashire. If the applicant seemed interested, however vaguely, in keeping children alive, that was a good sign. When you're barely twenty-three and have a third baby on the way, if your nanny likes children that's a bonus.

Living in an unfashionable place, ours was of course an unfashionable nursery. Our nearest smart, as in socially smart, neighbours were fifteen miles or more away or in fashionable Yorkshire. Burnley was hardly a draw. We had no title (my father was knighted later). The house was possibly even less comfortable and certainly less convenient than the houses the nannies had left behind. One good thing: my father brought them a glass of sherry every evening to cheer them up.

On reflection, I find it surprising that our nannies weren't Catholic. At least none came to Mass. Our Scrope cousins' nanny wasn't just Catholic, she was ferociously Catholic, taking it upon herself to oversee the governess's teaching of the Reformation to ensure no Protestant nonsense was peddled. Our nannies had to do Catholic things like oversee our pre-Mass fasting, organise the hot Ribena for fainting Oldest Sister and superintend our prayers. I'm not sure what any of them thought of being included in our prayers. Heaven being reserved for Catholics, we'd not meet them there if, that is, we made the grade ourselves. I was sometimes sorry about this.

Not sorry, though, for our first nanny. Nanny A. knew her business and her business was terror. A fierce Irish woman with fiercely asymmetrical hair and a fierce temper, she liked to punish what she saw as poor behaviour by throwing our cat, Snowy, out of the nursery window. I suppose she threw Snowy because she couldn't throw us, though the threat always hovered. For less serious waywardness she tied our hair with string and obliged us to stand in a corner wearing a punishment jersey, a scratchy coarse-wool cream-coloured object as I remember, with a head-hole so small it was like squeezing through the birth-canal (this was a later thought). When Second Sister threw up her porridge Nanny made her . . . I can't write it.

But just as Snowy took her defenestration in good part, so we accepted our penances. It never occurred to us not to. Nanny was queen of all she surveyed. And who would we have told? In those earliest nursery days we only saw our mother when Nanny was there, and though it's true that once a week my two older sisters and myself were dressed like dolls, shunted through the door that separated the nursery from the rest of the house and prodded down to the library so that our father could speak to us, it would never have occurred to us to tell him anything. At these meetings nobody spoke, our father regarding us with bemusement and we regarding him with unease. When the silence grew too awkward, he'd take his 'cello from its case and play until, to mutual relief, Nanny reeled us back upstairs. With the separating door firmly closed, her reign of terror continued.

When I was roughly four, Nanny A. took my two older sisters and me to Belfast where she had a sister of her own. This sister, so it turned out, ran a public house with rooms, some rented by the hour. The punters nodded respectfully to Nanny and were very polite to us. Some afternoons we visited a park filled with swans. Nanny declared, with meaning, that the swans had once pecked a little girl's head clean off. We held tightly onto our hats.

It's likely that my parents learned from somebody of the 'renting by the hour' because that, more than Nanny A.'s incipient madness, might have triggered concern. Anyhow, one day she was there and the next she wasn't. Our joy was tempered with dismay. Why had Nanny been shown the door instead of the window? More pertinently, without Nanny, who would look after us? We didn't want Nanny A. back but non-nanny days felt unsafe, jittery, spliced with the awful fear of being completely forgotten.

The relief when Nanny B. walked in must have been very pleasing to her. Perhaps she never guessed that her comfortable figure, green uniform, hair soft and thoroughly symmetrical, mattered much less than the restored routine and the regular sound of her knitting needles. With Nanny B. we were safe and so, we assumed, was Snowy. Actually, I have no memories of Snowy post-defenestration. Now I come to think of it, he may have been a she. He/she has no memorial. Unlike our many dogs, our cats never had their own burial ground. Their ends were seldom peaceful. Oldest Sister's kitten, named Selima after Thomas Gray's 'presumptuous maid' who drowned in a tub of goldfish, was eaten by an owl. Apart from hairy owl pellets, there was nothing left to bury.

Nanny B. ran a tight, not a mad, ship, and she wasn't a terrorist. True, she didn't encourage parental nursery visitations, something my father, apart from delivering Nanny's evening sherry, wouldn't have dreamed of in any event. If my mother wanted to visit the nursery she had to knock on the door and ask permission to enter. Since permission wasn't always granted, her enthusiasm waned. I'm not sure she minded. There was always another baby in the offing so in a way she carried the nursery with her. More important for everybody, Nanny B. set store by an orderly nursery and thus, in order, we rose, were dressed or dressed ourselves according to competence, said Grace, ate breakfast, brushed our teeth, went to the loo (our nannies were all obsessed by bowel movements), played, had elevenses, played, had lunch, rested, played, bathed, prayed and slept. When we played inside, we played under Nanny's watchful eye. When we played outside, we had complete freedom to kill ourselves so long as we inflicted no damage on the garden. I can see from photographs that Nanny came outside with the pram, but I think of her as an entirely inside creature.

It was during Nanny B.'s reign that I first properly met my father rather than observing him from a nervous distance.

Until judged fit company for the dining room, we children ate in the nursery. This was nothing to do with manners. We were better trained than circus poodles. Rather, my father feared we might be dull, a sin far more unforgiveable than using the wrong fork or even, his pet-hate, not using the butter knife. But one Sunday morning, some mishap diverting my parents, I was summoned from the nursery to the dining room to entertain the priest at breakfast. We sat opposite each other, the priest and I, at the table set up by the window, the breakfast laid by Carmello, our dazzle-buttoned butler. White tablecloth. Delicate breakfast china – brown leaf decoration I think. Cup and saucer, side plate, saucer on mat for egg-cup – always boiled eggs on Sundays. Silver knives, silver teaspoons, silver toast racks for the crustless, perfectly triangulated toast. Individual pats of butter perfectly centred on green leaf butter dishes, each pat stamped with our crest, a sparrowhawk, also perfectly centred. Small glass bowls of marmalade (home-made or Frank Cooper's) on special saucers, silver serving spoons lying beside. On the hotplate, the teapot, the coffeepot, the jug of hot milk, and the eggs, each silver egg-cup perfectly balanced in the round silver egg-cup holder, a contrivance I've never, to this day, seen anywhere else. Dining room breakfast was beautiful and you ate it beautifully, cracking the egg with a tender tap, buttering your toast a bite at a time. Tiny bites, tiny sips. Breakfast designed for the king and queen of the fairies.

This Sunday, for reasons I never discovered, I was part of the fairyness. I wasn't the queen, more a princess, and except for Carmello pouring tea and making sure the milk-jug was drip-free, I was alone with the priest. What did fairy princesses talk about? Flowers, I thought. I was untrained in flowers so couldn't think of anything flowery to say. The silence shrieked. Nobody wants to hear people buttering toast and Carmello, though emanating encouragement, couldn't help. It was with some desperation that I opened my mouth and out popped a question about drains. Were they always troublesome? How did they work? 'Ah, drains,' said the priest as if the topic wasn't remotely surprising at fairy breakfast. 'There's a lot to know about drains.' Carmello, smiling now, poured more tea and we did drains until breakfast was finished.

The meeting with my father came later that day. He told me that Father T. had complimented him on my perspicacity. What had we talked about?

'Drains,' I said.

'Why drains?'

'There's a lot to know about drains.'

My father looked at me, really looked, and I looked at him. 'I expect there is,' he said eventually. He couldn't bring himself then, or ever, to say 'well done'. Complimenting children led to the sin of pride, and pride was definitely on the slippery slope. He did, though, nod approvingly at Nanny. If a child of his could talk about drains to a priest at breakfast, she must be doing a decent job. I felt included in that nod. That nod made me happy.

Alas the twists of fate! One possible cause of Nanny B.'s eventual departure also involved me and my father. Her mistake? To despatch me along what we called my parents' passage to be beaten for the sin of breakfast-refusal. Breakfast was sheep's brains scraped from the sheep's head simmering on the Aga for the dogs. The brains were whitish-pink, oval-ish, a bit wrinkly, half-squashy, half-rubbery, with occasional stringy bits. Somehow, I didn't fancy them. Nanny didn't come with me on that long walk, at the end of which I found my father, his lower face slathered in shaving cream, floating misshapen foam-meringues in the shaving water. He was wearing pyjamas. This was startling. I imagined he'd be wearing a tie. He paused, shaving brush high. Through the cream he asked me my business. I stated it. He lowered the brush into the water and swished it about. The islands collided. We looked at them together. More swishing. More collisions.

He exchanged brush for razor. 'Do you like breakfast?'

'No.'

He pulled those faces men pull when shaving. 'I don't see why you should eat it then.'

Since that appeared to be that, I returned to the nursery. I never volunteered, and Nanny never asked, whether punishment had been inflicted. It hardly mattered. What mattered more was my father's belief that a nanny's most important duty was to keep children away from parents. If parents wished to see their children that was entirely up to them. Sending a child to a parent smacked of slippage. Slippage was doom. Nanny went soon after.

Her replacement, Nanny C., was the fattest person we'd ever seen, her hair oily enough to fry an egg. I thought she must have been raised in a cooking pot. She loved boys. Girls she hated, her concession being to allow my sisters and I the repulsive thrill of combing that oily hair along its tramlines of shiny scalp. When the combing novelty wore off we decided to murder her. Our method was simple, our weapon patience.

Our nursery and the nursery loo were at opposite ends of the nursery passage, each door visible from the other. The roof just inside the nursery door leaked. Given enough time, the rain soaked through to the plaster beneath. The plaster was Victorian and solid, but when the soaking reached a certain weight even the thickest plaster couldn't defy gravity and great gouts plummeted onto the carpet. We children were proficient ceiling-readers. We knew how to swerve the gouts. Nanny C. knew nothing of ceilings. If, when conditions were ripe, we could persuade her to stand where the gouts fell heaviest, she'd be floored, potentially fatally. This was Lancashire. We didn't have to wait long for rain, nor for the rain to steadily soak through the roof to the ceiling. When conditions were perfect, Second Sister stationed herself in the nursery loo. 'Nanny! Nanny! Come quick!' she cried. The urgency of the bawling meant Nanny could hardly not get up but we knew, being lazy, she'd stop by the nursery door. If she didn't need to walk further, she wouldn't. The nursery ceiling was poised. Nanny stopped in just the right place. We prayed. The ceiling duly collapsed. Every gout of plaster passed Nanny by. How was that possible? She was so large! It was harsh to learn that despite all our family had done for Him, God wouldn't do even this small thing for us.

Still, soon after that Nanny C. joined the burgeoning line of departure. Maybe she jaloused our murderous intentions and thought she might not be so lucky next time. Maybe it was because my brother bit her bottom. Maybe the evening glass of sherry wasn't generous enough. Whatever, she went and took her greasy comb with her. We didn't mourn.

Nanny D. had only one thing in common with mad Nanny A., stern Nanny B. and lucky Nanny C.: the pan-nanny horror of children eating oranges in any place except the bath. I was roughly twelve before I realised other people ate oranges at tables. It was a shock. In every other way Nanny D. was a novelty. For a start, she appeared to like us. She also loved to sing. At bathtime, marshalling us into a line facing the plug, she taught us her version of 'Poor Old Joe'.

> *Gone are the days when my heart was young and gay*
> *Gone from me to the cotton fields below*
> *Gone from me to a better land I know,*
> *I hear the gentle voices calling poor old Joe.*
> *I'm coming, I'm coming, with my head all bending low*
> *I hear the gentle voices calling poor old Joe.*

The song was mournful. Sometimes we cried. It only struck me later that a spiritual was an unlikely choice for a nanny who hailed from Stockport. Now I wish I'd known more about her. She had one drawback only but it was major. She was frail, and the Not-So-Grand house wasn't tolerant of frailty of any kind. I loved Nanny D.; I think the whole household did. But love her or not, for my mother, worn out by childbirth and fed-up with domesticity in a house so determinedly undomestic, frail wouldn't do. After a few nearly terminal 'frail days' Nanny D. left.

Then a miracle. Nanny E. arrived like an electrical charge. The moment she walked through the door, the house and all things in it, including people, leaped to their places and stood to attention.

From top to bottom, domestic quarrels were suspended, rivalries adjourned, tempers curbed. Even the plumbing seemed to pull itself together. Most miraculous of all, Nanny E. softened our father and saved our mother's life. She was the nanny we'd all been waiting for.

People who've never had a nanny believe that nannies should be cosy and fun. This is a myth. Nannies need three virtues: 1. to be dependably the same day in day out – no surprises; 2. to be utterly just and fair in their decisions; and 3. to have no discernible favourites. In addition, a good nanny is neither parental substitute nor confidential friend. She doesn't 'feel your pain'; she helps you endure it. She won't push the world one way or another; she'll keep your world on its axis so that when you're ready, you can step back in as though you'd never left. A good nanny doesn't need you to love her. Nursery life is not about her.

With wiry black hair, a flattish face, a broad downturned mouth and uncomforting hands, Nanny E. was the opposite of cosy. She was never fun. Instead, utterly fair, utterly just, utterly reliable, whether through training or instinct she emanated unassailable reassurance and safety. During Mass I didn't squeeze my hands so hard when Nanny E. was with us. If she couldn't stop a bomb (and if she couldn't, nobody could) she'd fix what came after. As for my mother, Nanny E. didn't save her by leaping into a river or carrying her from a burning building. She saved my mother by understanding, immediately and intuitively, that my mother was at her wits' end. Without comment, without judgement, without any sense of superiority and without either instruction from my mother or upsetting any of the tricksy characters already established in their domestic hierarchies, Nanny E. eased the Not-So-Grand house into running as smoothly, as cleanly, as silently as its peculiarities allowed. If she'd persuaded the plumbing to work, she would surely have been canonised.

On one of Nanny E.'s rare days off, Oldest Sister, long past nanny age, remembers sitting at the top of the front stairs gazing at the front door, willing it to grunt open and for Nanny E. to walk in so that everything would be its best self again. It wasn't that until Nanny E arrived the Not-So-Grand house had been an unhappy house. Not at all. It was just that Nanny E., not given to drama, steadied the ship and steered it round emerging rocks. When my mother, losing a baby, was stretchered out of the house to an ambulance, Nanny E. didn't try to pet us or play down our alarm. She got us through the day. When my mother returned, Nanny welcomed her in without fuss. We took our cue from her.

Her dealings with my father were masterly, and not through deferential manipulation. Where our welfare was concerned, she had tact but no fear. With greater or lesser forbearance, my father dropped us every morning at our primary school, insisting that lessons began at half-past nine because 'nothing starts before the end of the nine o'clock news'. This rubbish meant that every day we were late. Some days we were punished for it. When we dared, we begged him to reconsider. He reconsidered. 'Nothing starts before the end of the nine o'clock news.' Then came Nanny E. 'The children will be in the hall at twenty minutes to nine, sir,' she announced.

'Nothing starts before . . .'

'Twenty minutes to nine, sir. They'll be ready. They won't keep you waiting.'

My father opened his mouth. He shut it. We were never late again.

Home-time was trickier, even for Nanny E. In the tradition of all good nannies, she couldn't drive. Forbidden to travel on the bus (I don't know why), our collection was usually down to my mother. Unlike my father, she believed us when we told her that school ended at half-past three. She never meant to be late. It was just that she never looked at her watch. Some days, as time wore on, the nuns were reduced to rescuing us from the wall onto which we were glued, taking us in and giving us tea themselves. We would sit in their parlour, the nuns pretending not to mind, us pretending not to mind, everybody minding.

Perhaps instigated by Nanny E., from time to time Mr. S., the estate handyman, picked us up. The joy! There he was as we came out of school, all ready to sweep us onto his motorbike, one of us, helmetless, riding pillion and two of us bumping along cross-legged in the straw on the floor of his sidecar. The glamour! And there was more glamour. Very occasionally, Lord Savile, an old friend of my father's who also worshipped my mother, volunteered for collection duties. Like Mr. S., Lord Savile was never late. Even more exciting than the motorbike, he swept us into his Rolls-Royce, or was it a Bentley, and declared collecting us a treat. We felt like royalty. Most days, though, it was the long wait.

From sitting on that waiting wall I did learn an important lesson: as most of life is waiting, never go anywhere without a book. I also swore that if I had children I'd never ever be late picking them up. It took three children before I realised that I had in fact turned into my mother. Lacking Nanny E., Mr. S. or a friendly peer, the only solution was to move house so the children could walk. When I told my mother, she laughed. 'I suppose I was occasionally late,' she said. I laughed then. Nanny E. would have laughed too. She didn't laugh often, but when she did, she LAUGHED.

Nanny E. was our last nanny. After a stroke diminished her physical powers, when she came to the Not-So-Grand house for visits, roles were reversed: we looked after her. She was always happiest in the nursery and would sit and wait patiently for one of us, long past nursery age, to sit with her for a while. She accepted our ham-fisted help, the embarrassment on both sides acknowledged and brushed off with a lopsided smile. Every evening, my father brought her a glass of sherry just as he always had. She took it and thanked him, and he said 'how are you, Nan,' – he always called her 'Nan' – and she said 'I'm very well, sir'. In his presence, for a moment, her confident, brisk orderliness would return. Then it would subside slowly into a gentle stillness except that her fingers still moved, habitually searching for knitting needles or darning needles, or nametapes to sew on or hems to stitch. As her memory waxed and waned she would chat about her 'other family', very smart people whom she had served for many years before us. Caring for their three boys, she'd been to America and all over the shop. Good nannies make bad gossips so we learned nothing about this 'other family' apart from what could be read in newspapers. Whatever, we didn't like them. So far as I know, they didn't visit Nanny.

After dinner was Nanny E.'s favourite time of all. It was then that even with a myriad other things pressing, slowly and with infinite patience my mother would give Nanny a bath. This bath wasn't just water and soap. It was the purest manifestation of love and respect I've ever seen: easing Nanny out of clothes, easing her into the tub, chatting, reminiscing, everything unhurried, time unbegrudged. That was Nanny's last gift to us, that we could witness this love and respect, hers for our mother, our mother's for her. We could witness it, and when our mother was ill and couldn't bath Nanny herself, we could move into her place and Nanny would feel our love too.

These role-reversal days were strange. We sat or moved quietly in the once humming nursery, both reassured by Nanny's presence – reassurance was engrained – and unsettled. Obviously we didn't need a nanny any more. Yet as our lives tipped and turned, we more than ever needed Nanny E. to be in the world. To lose her would be like losing a tree. Your life would move along but the loss would matter, and we knew the loss was coming.

My mother wasn't with Nanny E. when she died. She sat by Nanny's hospital bed for three days and nights, left momentarily to get a cup of tea and returned to find Nanny dead. A nurse leaned over, shouting, as if Nanny could be woken up. My mother was distraught. She took Nanny's hand and gave the nurse a scolding. Nanny would have smiled, and though my mother tried to be comforted by that thought, I'm not sure she ever was.

In the Not-So-Grand house, Nanny's room remains Nanny's room. All attempts not to call it Nanny's room end in failure. The wallpaper has changed, though even the 'new' wallpaper is now so mottled you'd never guess. When I go home, I sometimes sleep in Nanny's bed. I don't really like it. Decades since any of our nannies slept there, the room still feels reserved for someone who isn't me. As children we wouldn't have dreamt of so much as opening the door. I find it easier to sleep in what was our night-nursery, sinking back into the days of Nanny D.'s Poor Old Joe and Nanny E. singing 'good morning merry sunshine' as she swished the curtains open. Here I catch glimpses of me and my sisters in a row, our clothes neatly laid out, Nanny bustling about the morning's business, the day stretching ahead. In these snatches the sun is indeed merry, and I'm flooded by one of those sudden rushes of uncomplicated childhood happiness more powerful than any photograph. Photographs are static. This feeling is a wave.

I don't resist. One moment I'm washed back onto the rocking chair opposite the nursery bookcase. The next I'm opening the dressing up drawer whose contents – the opera cloak, the pink gauze ballet skirt, the floppy 1920s hats, the bedraggled fur stoles, the top hat, the mothy velvet slippers – lent our favourite 'let's pretend' games a certain elegance.

And now I've washed up somewhere else. It's 1988 and I've brought my first baby down to the Not-So-Grand house to stay with her grandparents for a week whilst I go away. My father has insisted that his granddaughter be accompanied by a nanny, a Norland nanny[*] indeed, whose salary he will pay. A Norland nanny duly appears. Here she is in her smart Norland uniform, popping the baby into the enormous Not-So-Grand house Silver Cross pram. Before I leave, I help steady the pram down the pram-ramp which has been dusted off and resettled into its old place on the steps leading into the garden from the north door. Off Norland Nanny goes, pushing the pram on its freshly oiled wheels into the sunshine.

We watch, my father, my mother and I. Though we exchange not a word, we can see all the nannies who pushed that pram. We're smiling, or almost smiling. It's true that nannies can pull families apart. It's also true that the Not-So-Grand house nannies,

* https://www.norland.ac.uk/employing-a-norland-nanny/

notwithstanding their quirks and foibles, each in their own way pulled us together. Whatever letting go I must do now, I mustn't let go of that.

9

THE DEAD AND THE 'DEAD'

W E CALLED MY father's mother 'Granny' but don't be fooled. Granny wasn't cosy. We didn't have a paternal grandfather. Well, we did, but Granny loathed the father of her children so much that she led us to believe he was dead. It was only after asking our father the identity of the man who once came to stay at home that we learned that our grandfather wasn't dead in the usual sense. He was simply dead to Granny and, in every sense that mattered, dead to my father, and so, although he was in the dining room having breakfast, dead to us. 'Should we call him Dead Grandpapa?'

'Call him whatever you like.'

'What do you call him?'

'I don't call him anything.'

It wasn't clear what a man so clearly alive had done to be deemed so namelessly dead. It's hard to ask dead people anything. The story seems to be this.

Our paternal great grandfather, Alexander Koch de Gooreynd, a Belgian banker but naturalised Englishman, was, according to my uncle Perry Worsthorne, 'quite eager to make the grade in English society'. He was also a Catholic, so the marriage of his son, another Alexander (always known as Lexie, so, in the end, we discovered) to my grandmother, granddaughter of the Earl of Abingdon and his wife, Caroline neé Towneley of Towneley, was, like my parents', a match made in Catholic heaven. More illustriously Catholic still, my grandmother's Aunt May was married to Viscount FitzAlan, brother of the Duke of Norfolk and a friend of King George V and Queen Mary. Even heavenly blue-blood wasn't enough to glue bride and bridegroom together. Lexie, rich and indolent, and Granny, high-minded and serious, had no interests in common. To give them at least a common cause, it was suggested that Lexie stand for Parliament for the constituency of Farnworth in Lancashire. The surname Koch de Gooreynd, its first part ribald, its second unpronounceable and the whole unquestionably foreign, wouldn't do, so my grandfather was persuaded to adopt the name Worsthorne, a village on the Towneley estates belonging to his mother-in-law. The moment the voters of Farnworth rejected him, Lexie discarded Worsthorne and resumed Koch de Gooreynd. My grandmother, always contrary, kept Worsthorne and discarded Lexie. At a stroke, he was 'dead' and she never spoke his name again.

If only Granny had been a wild and glamorous Bolter like Fanny's mother in Nancy Mitford's *The Pursuit of Love*! Instead, bolting was left to my 'dead' grandfather. He married at least twice more. After he really did die, at his funeral we addressed every woman of a certain age as Mrs K de G since it seemed likely the name either was, or had been, theirs.

Granny went further than discarding her husband. With astonishing vindictiveness, she cut her children off not just from their father but from his whole family. Contact was allowed only through a solicitor, any infractions treated as treason. For a while, treason appealed to my grandfather. It amused him to turn up at his sons' school in a Rolls-Royce with a hamper full of foie-gras and caviar, a captivating paramour in tow. Treason lost its sparkle. The Rolls-Royce never appeared again and nor, in my father and uncle's childhood, did he. This would have mattered less had Granny been a warm and loving mother. She was not. Had it been allowed, she'd have stuck 'return to sender' labels on my father and uncle particularly after she caught the eye of Montagu Norman, then Governor of the Bank of England. Twenty years her senior and never previously married, it was an unexpected match which Granny embraced with religious fervour. Such was the Governor's importance, the marriage hit the newspaper headlines and my father and uncle learned of it from a billboard they spotted from the top of a bus. When Granny finally told them herself, she never forgave my eleven year old father for exclaiming 'I thought you were already married!' And of course in the eyes of the Catholic Church she was, so this marriage to Montagu Norman generated yet another discarding. Not only did my great-grandmother and all our English Catholic relations not recognise Granny's divorce, she was now marrying a PROTESTANT.

Added to no more visits to the Koch de Gooreynds in Belgrave Square were no more Christmases with Uncle Edmund and Aunt May Fitzalan at Cumberland Lodge with the king and queen dropping in for tea. No more stays with Norfolk cousins at Arundel Castle, where it was Granny's habit to tell her sons not to eat too much because 'the Norfolks are very poor, you know'. There was also no more home. Granny sold the London house in which she and the boys lived, Granny on one floor, her children on another, and they all moved into Montagu Norman's house, Thorpe Lodge in Notting Hill. I say 'they all moved' but really Granny moved. Although they were to call Montagu Norman 'Uncle Mont', her children were not to consider Thorpe Lodge as 'home'. The boys were visitors, allowed over the threshold on sufferance. At the Norman country house, St. Clere, they weren't even allowed over the threshold. Refusing any welcome the Normans wanted to extend, Granny sent my father and uncle to live in a house down the road. It was a delightful house, with a tutor, a housekeeper, ponies and all kinds of amusements, so what could be wrong with that? If Uncle Mont happened to bump into the boys, he'd offer 'hope you've had enough grub'. I don't think there was much point in saying 'no'. After Uncle Mont died, without so much as a nod to irony, Granny took up the cause of mental health, particularly child mental health and child guidance. In this she had a distinguished career as a board member of the Maudsley Hospital as well as president of this and that. An owl in charge of dormice.

You might have thought that, once grown up, my father would have done his own discarding and rejected his mother. But it was our father's misfortune that although Granny's 'return to sender' label hovered until she died in 1991, he wanted her to love him. Perhaps like would have been enough. He just wanted something. Granny could feel this wanting and resented it, and he resented her resenting him, so they were like nettles in each other's presence, the least brush making the other flinch and scowl. Such was the discomfort between them that Granny's visits to the Not-So-Grand house were tense as a hostile invasion. Everything had to be planned – what to eat, what to drink, whom to ask to dinner, what to do. Nothing was left to chance.

'Lady Norman is coming this week,' my father might announce to Nanny at breakfast. If Granny was to arrive on Tuesday, my father would start flinching on roughly Sunday. The Not-So-Grand house, alerted by the flinching, would respond by ratcheting up its peculiarities and inconveniences. Lightbulbs would pop, doorhandles fall off. The roof would spring new leaks. The Aga would sulk and the septic tank, silent for the rest of the year, would hiss with eruptive menace.

All in all, I can't see why Granny came. She had no affection for the place. She particularly disliked the oratory, a needling reminder that despite having been married to Montagu Norman for nearly two decades, and him being dead for another two, the Catholic church still considered her married to our 'dead' grandfather. Offended by the wiggly way in which, through her grandmother, then her cousin, then her mother, then her, the estate and the Not-So-Grand house had landed on my father's lap, she professed to despise inheritance. In her view, inheritance bred sloth. Decades after my father had established himself in the county, she still radiated disappointment and disapproval, as if he'd given up a stellar career in something or other for sitting around and doing nothing at all.

In the 'nothing at all' stakes she did find common cause with us children. At primary school, we were always having to write compositions titled 'what your father does'. What did our father do? Apart from guarding against slippage, so far as we were aware he didn't 'do' anything, certainly nothing recognisable in a school composition. We asked our mother. She didn't seem sure. We asked Nanny. She sniffed. Fathers were men. He did what men do which, in her experience, was to be men. We were stumped. After much debate and disagreement, we decided to ask our father what was on his passport. 'Gentleman,' he said. In the end, we agreed to write that our father had 'no occupation' which, in the parlance of the day, meant he was in jail. Since we saw little of him, at least elements of that were true.

A small aside: it wasn't true that our 'dead' grandfather had done nothing. Firstly there were all those marriages, one to a thrilling Russian countess, another to a wife by whom he'd fathered another son. He had been in the Irish Guards, an MP in Rhodesia (as it was then), and a big enough noise in horse-racing in Salisbury (now Harare) to have a race named 'The Worsthorne Cup' (the Koch de Gooreynd Cup doesn't flow off the tongue). He'd also contrived to lose all his money, an achievement of sorts as he started off with so much. During a jolly dinner much later, my father told me that Lexie had, for a while, been the third part of a ménage à trois. Seems quite a lot to me.

Perhaps I never really understood how deeply Granny's dislike of my father bit into his soul until small anecdotes occasionally burst from him, the shame, as he saw it, of wanting to confide, all tangled up with his extraordinarily unwavering filial loyalty. Usually the only listeners were us, his children, but one anecdote was shared in surprising company.

A member of the Royal Family, a friend of my father's and an admirer of my mother's, had come to visit my mother's grave in the churchyard at St. Hubert's, Dunsop Bridge.

'Come in for a cup of tea,' said the parish priest, more than a little nonplussed to find a princess amongst the tombstones.

'Just what's needed, Father,' the princess said with a charmingly royal smile. Into the presbytery we all trooped and sat down on the big brown furniture all presbyteries seem to breed.

Picking up small artefacts from his big brown sideboard and asking their provenance, the princess put Father C. at his ease. Despite the inevitable hesitations, clumsinesses and inadvertent clatterings that go with giving a royal a cup of tea, Father soon lost his 'oh crikey, royalty' stammer. Some of the little artefacts had been presents, and to reciprocate Father C.'s sketches of the givers – he was a brilliant mimic – the Royal told of the lavender bags the Queen Mother made herself and handed out as small very personal gifts – a lovely story.

My father put down his teacup with a slight bang. 'When we made presents for our mother, if she didn't like them she curled her lip, sniffed "how kind", and later we'd find them back on our beds,' he said. There was silence. Even princesses can be disconcerted. Crikey crikey crikey. My siblings and I blinked madly at each other. Was this a 'rescue' situation? If so, what form should rescue take? Father C. rose. Oh Lord, I thought. He's going to offer my father sympathy. My father would growl. He might even snarl. And then what? But Father C. hadn't been a parish priest for decades without learning a thing or two. He picked up the teapot. 'More tea?' Just as he knew we would, we all said yes quite loudly.

That Granny's meanness could break through my father's usual carapace at even the most inappropriate of times shook me. Before that moment, I suppose I hadn't thought much about how, if the relationship between mothers and sons is poisoned or simply doesn't work, whereas for the mother (if she's not Granny) that's a sadness, for the son it's an untreated sore. The evening of the outburst I wanted to say something, I don't know what. Obviously not sympathy. Just something. My father was reading but I sensed he was also poised, armour on. I got as far as 'Granny really was' – before he cracked his book shut. 'I'm going upstairs to say my prayers,' he said, and vanished. By the time he came down for dinner, both evening and conversation had moved on. We never referred to the outburst again. Pointless to regret that now.

My mother's relationship with her mother-in-law was as simple as my father's was complicated. For roughly a decade after marriage, my mother tried to please. Then she snapped. She'd driven down from Lancashire, motorways hardly invented, and arrived at the flat into which Granny had moved after Uncle Mont's death ten minutes later than she'd estimated. Deeming herself inconvenienced, Granny locked the flat door. My mother spent the night in the car. The following morning, Granny expected an apology. She got an explosion. She crumpled. A lucky crumpling since towards the end of her life Granny depended on my mother for all her solace and comfort, and my mother never let her down.

Unbeknownst to Granny, when we were grown up my siblings and I occasionally visited Lexie. He'd ended up in Elm Park Gardens, eking out a solitary existence in two tiny rooms allocated to the 'genteel destitute' supported, I imagine, by his Irish Guards pension. He was always surprised to be visited. There was tea if we made it ourselves. No biscuits. His cupboards were bare. It was a long way from hampers, paramours and Belgrave Square and really, he felt a long way from us. This didn't bother him. We were grandchildren in name only. Shortly before he died, Lexie wrote to my uncle Perry the only letter he sent to either of his sons. In his *Tricks of Memory* Perry records the text: 'I have done nothing with my life but possibly my example spurred you on to do something with yours. It pleases me to think so. It is too late now for us ever to talk – this note will have to do instead'[*].

It wasn't too late, not quite, but they didn't talk and soon our 'dead to Granny' grandfather was dead to us all. His funeral was the funeral of a stranger. Sad, though. Grandfathers aren't two a'penny.

As for Granny, you couldn't fault her interest in us, her

[*] Worsthorne, P., 1993, *Tricks of Memory*, Weidenfeld & Nicolson, p.193.

grandchildren. She visited. She took us on holidays. She gave generous Christmas presents. Always judgemental, always keen to hurt my father, she was hard to love. I felt guilty about that. You're supposed to love your granny. Our mistake, I see now, was to think of her as a grandmother, just as our father's mistake was to think of her as a mother, and Lexie's was to think of her as a wife. Really, she was just one of those women who, with an odd twist of chemistry, makes everybody uncomfortable. I can let go of Granny without a qualm. Uncomfortable people are better parked at a distance.

10

AVOIDING TWEED

MY TWO OLDER sisters' governess, Miss S., wore tweed skirts and was a certain age. Every week she was joined by two other tweed skirts to form a string quartet with my father. The Lead Tweed was Mrs B. Miss S. played the viola. I can't remember the name of the Tweed who played second violin – namelessness is often the fate of second violins, particularly tweedy ones. Before the house was extended, the quartet played in the hall behind the door, top half astragalled, bottom half solid, so they appeared as tweedy squares. After the house was extended they played in the drawing room and Carmello took in the tea-tray at the appointed time. My father only liked tea at breakfast but tea was important to the Tweeds and the Tweeds were important to my father, ergo, tea. He didn't encourage cake.

Had my father not dedicated his life to 'no more slippage', music might have been his focus. He was a keen and dedicated 'cellist, fond of recounting how, aged sixteen or seventeen, he'd suggested to his 'cello teacher that he'd like to play professionally. 'Oh,' she exclaimed, 'if only I'd known, I'd have taught you entirely differently.' And that, according to my father, was that. A true vocation, and he'd have resisted, persisted, insisted. Actually, the closing of the professional door suited him. Being a professional involves trying. To him, trying, and certainly being seen to try, smacked of the slippery slope. When he practised his 'cello he was not trying. What he was doing we never knew, only that it was something quite different. What we did when we practised our instruments was trying in both senses of that word, so if we weren't to irritate my father we had to try neither to try nor be trying.

Despite the trying muddle, in the Not-So-Grand house music was everywhere. There was the music our nurserymaids were mad about: the Hollies, the Beatles, Acker Bilk's 'Stranger on the Shore' always battling the relentless crackle of wireless static. There was music from the thick vinyl records we played on the blue and white nursery gramophone that never had a new needle: the Browns 'The Three Bells', Caruso singing arias, Peter and the Wolf – all, so I first believed, created by His Master's Voice's dog. We could listen to these without Nanny scurrying to close the nursery door to keep the sound in. My father would never have considered the Beatles music.

A new record arrived one Christmas, addressed to all of us. On one of those out-of-time days between Christmas and the New Year when even in the Not-So-Grand house the boundary between the nursery and the front-of-house blurred, my mother popped the record onto the smart radiogram that sat outside my father's library door. At the first bars of Scott Joplin's Maple Leaf Rag my father emerged. He looked at us and we at him. Somehow we all began to dance. The music being unfamiliar and its syncopation funny, we boogied as I imagine ducks might boogie, bumping into each other, quacking slightly. On second playing the rags seemed full of stories, some melancholy, some slapstick, and we danced jerkily, like characters in a Charlie Chaplin film. Somebody turned up the volume so we could hop down the hall, down the passage, past the gents, down the steps and round the drawing room. The oratory curtain shimmied. I thought that might stop my father in his tracks. The slippery slope! But my father and mother, both laughing and flushed, continued to move together as I'd never seen them move before. We danced out of the drawing room. When the radiogram needle slid towards the spindle for the third time my father replaced the arm on the armrest and we dropped our own arms and looked about us, not quite believing what had just happened. The world of the Not-So-Grand house shook slightly. It re-settled. Still, the slippery slope had threatened, and my father had danced on.

From string quartets, something different. I don't mean the Tweeds. I mean exotics from far away countries whose visits heralded a flurry of concerts and parties and who, to a man – they were always men – loved children. When musicians love children, children love music. It's an entirely natural trade-off.

The quartets began unpromisingly. My father was President of the Mid-Pennine Association for the Arts (now Mid Pennine Arts), whose goal, turgid as porridge, was to 'increase the accessibility of the fine arts and dramatic art to the public throughout the Mid-Pennine area' and to 'build up an audience for one form of music'[*]. Quartets were chosen as the 'one form' because the performance space, namely the Burnley Library, was limited. How the individual quartets were approached and why they, world-famous, chose to accept invitations to Burnley I don't know. I only know that when they walked through the front door of the Not-So-Grand house, smiling, nodding, their English often almost zero, along with music they brought enchantment.

The first enchantment was the Borodin depositing their priceless instruments like so much baggage so they could bend to our level to say 'hello, hello' as though they'd travelled all this way just for us. After the Borodin came the Smetana and the Prague, the Amadeus and many more. We knew nothing of their legendary status. All we knew was that their presence sharpened the air as before theatre curtain-up, except there was no scrim dividing us from them and they had no notion of slippery slopes.

Unaware that there was any division between the front of the

---

[*] Doris Nield Chew, *A Venture in the Arts: The Mid-Pennine Association for the Arts 1966–1978*

http://midpenninearts.org.uk/wp-content/uploads/2016/04/A-VENTURE-IN-THE-ARTS-MD-draft-with-images-v.1.pdf, [accessed 14 August 2023] house and the back, in breaks from rehearsing the musicians found the nursery. Unaware, too, of nursery rules, they wandered in. 'Come downstairs,' they coaxed. 'Come down.' Snared by their broken English and melancholy smiles, Nanny was helpless. So down we went, into the drawing room where the music was. Here was no sepulchral reverence. Here was music as delight, music that spoke.

It never occurred to my parents that we were too young for the concerts. Who can be too young for delight? Who can be too young for music that speaks? With progressive intuition, my father sat us right at the front of the concert hall, very near the quartet. Often, amid the applause, the quartet would bow specially to us and we, dressed in our best clothes, bowed back, all part of the performance.

After the concert, the Not-So-Grand house filled with dinner guests, the dining room softly candle-lit, everything beautiful in the way my mother could make things beautiful, and she herself beautiful and overflowing with hospitality. My father, too, full of the music and also overflowing with hospitality, forgot about slippage, about the sourness of Granny, about anything beyond the rich enjoyment of evenings that drew the whole household together. Even Nanny was drawn to the dining room. If I think of 'the days of our lives', these are them, those evenings: the glow, the joy, the shared enchantment.

When we were older, for some years my father took a selection of daughters with him to the Dartington Summer School for a week of music and cream teas. Just as when my parents went to Venice my father and his 'cello travelled first class and my mother second, so on trips to Dartington his 'cello travelled in the front seat of the car, the selection of daughters in the back. Unlike our boarding school journeys, this wasn't a journey made on sufferance – what a nuisance, having to take children anywhere. With music in the offing my father was relaxed, expansive, and perhaps because his 'cello was his neighbour and he couldn't see us except in the mirror, one year – I was perhaps twelve or thirteen – he spoke of his visit to Bayreuth the year Wagner's Festspielhaus reopened after the war. He stayed with a German couple, strangers to him, who advertised bed and breakfast. In the drawer of the desk in his room he found the framed photograph of a young German officer in full Nazi uniform. The boy was proud, smiling. There was a space for the photograph above the fireplace but no sign in the room of life. He replaced the picture in the drawer, face down, as he'd found it. The silence in the car that followed this revelation was different from other car silences: contemplative, not combative. I could imagine my father replacing the photograph. For the rest of the journey I wondered about the memories people carry with them, and how chancy it is that they ever emerge. I wanted him to say more but didn't know how to ask. The silence remained unbroken. Eventually, I suppose I fell asleep and the moment, like so many others, passed.

We broke the long drive roughly halfway down, overnight, with cousins. Their daughter was midst O' levels and she, unstudious, revealed she was getting £5 for every O' level gained. She was hoping for £15 or so, she said. My father, still in relaxed and expansive mood and having no idea either of O' levels or his children's academic abilities, said he'd do the same. His shock when, in time, he was presented with bills at least three times larger than expected was very satisfactory. He paid up without complaint. With some of my money I bought a record-player of my own. The miracle of Leonard Cohen, Queen and David Bowie with no radio static! I bought very few classical records. For that kind of music I wanted living, breathing players.

The organic warmth of live music wasn't the quartets' only legacy: I learned from watching their drawing room practice that on the trying front my father was entirely wrong. If, with music, you don't try, you play with tweedy ladies. I've nothing against tweedy ladies. With their sensible hairdos, sensible shoes and sensible views, tweedy ladies are the backbone of civilisation. But honestly and truly, if you've any choice in the matter, do you want to end up tweedy yourself?

11

DO NOT DISTURB

R EADING CAME MORE easily than riding a bicycle. I'd seen Oldest Sister and Second Sister learning with a governess in the dining room and thought Nanny probably knew about reading so I asked her to teach me. By the time I was five, hours could pass when I heard nothing, saw nothing, was aware of nothing except the life of my book. It wasn't an escape from home. I didn't want to escape. I just wanted to be in other worlds too, and there they were, between the covers, waiting for me. How books could make you suffer! The injustices, mainly, but not always, resolved. The losses characters endured. The elation; devastation; terror; joy. What happiness when things worked out. What wrenching sadness when they didn't. Reading was my drug. I couldn't get enough of it. Writing arrived later and was intimately connected to the hard-backed notebook.

Our primary school nuns decreed that you couldn't have a hard-backed notebook until you could form your letters neatly with a pencil. We did a lot of tracing in soft-backed notebooks. After tracing came copying letters from the blackboard, letters Sister MB slowly described out loud: '"a" starts on the line, up and round, then back and down and round, well not quite round, and up and catch that line, then down and loop'. Sister MB came to inspect. On her inspection depended your graduating from soft-backed to hard-backed.

The hard-backed notebooks had blue-marbled covers and pages that made rustly thin-paper noise yet were sturdy enough to keep ink from bleeding. They were like gifts from heaven, only here they were on earth. The tension surrounding Sister MB's letter inspection was enough to make you die.

I can still feel the pit-of-stomach thrill when my first hard-backed book landed on my desk. I opened it with reverence. Its pale red margins and pale blue lines were perfect. I shut it. I opened it. I shut it again. Incomparable feelings of bliss.

I picked up my pen, and with it the awful, inescapable knowledge that at the first touch of nib on paper my book would be spoiled. The pen wouldn't immediately smudge. I'd not immediately make a spelling mistake. My letters might not be flawless but they'd be letters. The book would be spoiled simply because I'd marked it. The bliss flipped into something like grief. I had to grit my teeth to perform the marking deed. As soon as I'd done it, I wanted to tear out the spoiled page and pretend the notebook was still untouched. A torn notebook isn't a perfect notebook, but after that first spoiling it's as near as you're going to get. Tearing pages from your notebook was forbidden so once I'd been forced to make a mark, usually writing my name with the disquieting conundrum of those 'ees', the notebook would remain spoiled forever more. For a day I'd be upset. Every time I opened the book I'd truly suffer. Sometimes I prayed that I'd open the book and it would be pristine again or that Sister MB would forget she'd already given me a hard-backed book and hand out another.

Yet the spoiling was also relief. You can only spoil something once, and after it's spoiled, it's just a thing. For a time, that's what my hard-back booked was, a spoiled thing. Yet once enough pages had been filled, enough ticks and crosses neatly or not so neatly assigned by heedless teachers, enough blots had blotted, enough apple-cores had stuck, enough corners had dogeared and it had brushed up against who-knows-what in my satchel, I found one day that the notebook and I had moved on. No longer were we the spoiled and the spoiler: we'd become comrades-in-arms. Now we shared struggles and compared battle-scars, particularly where sums were concerned. I began to eke out the diminishing pages. When no pages were left, I found saying goodbye a tug, not as wrenching as saying goodbye to a dog, more on the level, say, of a rabbit or a guineapig.

Since spoiling those blue-marble hard-backed notebooks of my primary school I've spoiled a lot of things, including a lot of other notebooks. Mostly, these days, I don't bother to use the word 'starting' as in 'starting a new notebook'. For almost everything 'spoiling' is much more accurate. Also, since primary school, I've never bought another blue-marbled hard-backed book. I've picked them up, even hovered over them on Amazon, but I've never bought one. Like first loves, hard-backed books should remain unrevisited.

Reading carried no spoiling taint. Rather the opposite. In 1964 the portrait artist John Norton came to paint Oldest Sister, Second Sister and me. We were taken downstairs to my mother's sitting room to meet him. There it was explained that we would be required to sit (me, Eldest Sister) or stand (Second Sister) for a very long time or the whole thing would be ruined.

On appointed days Nanny dressed each of us in velvet frocks, smoothed the closely pleated lace collars and cuffs and tied our wide satin sashes in firm bows. Eldest Sister's dress was brown, Second Sister's blue and mine green though John Norton painted it orange, I don't know why. Artists take an age to prep before putting their brush on the canvas so I took my book to my sittings and put it down only when instructed. Later, whilst brushes were changed and palettes cleaned, I stood up, and because nobody told me not to, returned to my book. In the finished painting, I saw my orange sitting self, the self the artist had been commissioned to paint, and behind, there I was again, a second self, my 'real' self as I thought and still think, a shadowy standing figure, a reader reading. It was my first compliment.

Staying with friends, it came as a surprise that a house full of books isn't always a house full of reading. I still find it shocking that some people consider reading 'doing nothing'. In the Not-So-Grand house, reading was most definitely doing something. As with praying, you didn't disturb somebody who was reading. In the front of the house, the silence of my father reading in his library was solid and unshakeable: silence as sound. Noises did intrude – Mrs N. chirruping; Mrs C. hoovering; the telephone ringing. But the silence, like the dust, soon settled again. Silence wasn't a rule. Nobody said 'be quiet'. Yet never, as a child or at any time later, did I walk through the front door to be greeted by noise.

Human noise, that is. The house itself was permanently complaining. The front door passage wailed like a banshee when the wind was in the east and there was always a steady clip of drips from leaks now here, now there. Even on windless days the windows rattled. Through the cold tap in the spare bathroom the house liked to blast a full-blown cannonade of snorts, grunts and burps in protest at the presence of guests. A silent house can also be a noisy house.

And the reading silence was strictly front-of-house. Behind the equivalent of the green-baize door, in those back spaces where the household leant their shoulders to the domestic wheel, there was no place for reading silence or, for that matter, any silence at all. Cooks of varied tempers cajoled and scolded. Nurserymaids, noisily happy or noisily unhappy, stomped up and down the back stairs bearing trays and nappy buckets. Mrs N. chatted whilst she drank her brew. There were deliveries in vans from Hargreaves the Grocers, and sometimes, echoing through the kitchen window, the mournful, tinny cry of the rag-and-bone man, the totter, with his skinny horse trying his luck.

During the Carmello years of my early childhood, the back space noise was considerably increased by his wife Rosa, employed, perhaps unwillingly, as one of those variedly tempered cooks. Carmello, kind, self-effacing, worked with quiet precision, checking his uniform carefully before taking up his duties. Rosa was the opposite. Excitable and volatile, she pitched in full throttle, waving knives, clattering pans, everything a commotion. The day she made pizza my mother summoned us all down to witness its emergence from the Aga. The colours! The smell! The flatness! I'd never seen anything like it. It was my first conscious meeting with an olive. We ate slices without plates, us chattering, my mother chattering, Rosa chattering, our delight reflected in Rosa's delight at our delight. Pizza in hand, my mother, who spoke Italian, and Rosa, who spoke no English, conjured a momentary flash of a clamorous Sicilian street, an audible glimpse of sunshine in a Lancashire kitchen shadowed by dripping trees. I was aware of other-ness, or foreign-ness, and how both Rosa and my mother had ended up somewhere that wasn't them. I didn't know what that meant, and not knowing, and finding not knowing disturbing, I ate my pizza cautiously.

Rosa came to the front of the house only at Christmas. Rather more subdued, she and her family, first one, then two, then three boys, all dressed in their good clothes, were given their presents. One year, in my mind the pizza year, there was a panic. The oldest boy had swallowed a rosary. The pearl-smooth rosary beads were shrugged off as normal fare for Catholic children. Not so the pointy crucifix. The boy wasn't a python. How on earth had he swallowed that? Rosa was beside herself; the boy himself unmoved. The eventual hospital scan revealed the miraculous safe passage of the crucifix, one amongst many elements of the boy's varied diet of the edible and inedible, the secular and religious. Also pizza. I was impressed. I also felt I was right to be cautious.

It strikes me now that the Not-So-Grand house silence wasn't only for reading. In the silence we listened for footsteps. If Nanny's footsteps were brisk but not hurried and the nurserymaid's hurried but not brisk, all was well. My father's footsteps were always brisk, the sound enough to straighten backs: brace, brace. If, as sometimes happened, my mother had forgotten to take off her gumboots, her footsteps were squeaky. Mainly, though, hers were the swift, soft, stocking-feet pad of the permanently late. She never learned to walk, let alone run, in heels.

When Second Sister and I graduated to the attic bedroom, footsteps were often drowned out by the water tank, another sulky Methuselah like the Aga except noisier, and just beyond, equally noisy, its sidekick, the 'it's always been here' attic loo. That loo. Almost hidden amongst lamps with no bases, bases with no lamps, beds with no springs, springs with no beds, horsehair mattresses, portraits of dead people, Victorian mourning dresses, leaves for tables long since extinct, cots, cradles, ladies fans, commodes, boxes of candles 'with one hour to burn' and bits of furniture too ugly even for children's bedrooms, it was really more theatre props cupboard. Decades of peace disturbed by our arrival, we found ourselves in stiff competition with the mice. Over time we added to the loo's theatrical clutter a copy of one of the Towneley marbles – a girl, naked except for a Chinese hat we found for her – and an antique television set, innards poking out,

How I loved that attic. How I loved that loo. I'll never let go of that love. Even now, when I'm ill or gloomy I imagine myself back there, the light speckled green in summer, brownish orange in autumn and slate grey in winter. At night, the munching and sighing of the cows in the field beyond the trees crowded uncannily close, and the owl, hunting and hooting in the trees, made you glad you weren't a vole. Beyond trees and field and main road, occasional goods trains chuntered along the railway, jangling like some knight shaking out his armour. What can the trains have been doing? I've still no idea.

Cut off from the rest of the house by a set of steep stairs, up here Second Sister and I could safely read Enid Blyton, forbidden downstairs, and the entirety of Malory Towers. After Second Sister left for boarding school, for most of the year the attic was my *Room of One's Own*. In a room of one's own, one can make one's own amusements.

For my First Communion, Nanny D. had given me a missal. Small, with crinkly pages and *The Key of Heaven* inscribed in gold on its mother-of-pearl cover, in my solo attic fastness my new game was to read Mass aloud, in Latin, including the Gospel, in direct contravention of all the rules that forbad girls even to say Amen. Hearing myself recite what the priest alone recited and, even more, hearing myself reciting my father's responses, was major sedition. I sometimes worried that it was also a major sin. Still, I declaimed the forbidden whilst the water tank fulminated and the loo grumbled.

Later, older, something else. From the passage directly below the attic I grew so used to the jolty jigger jigger of the laundry pulley descending and eventually, even more jerkily, ascending, that it only made an impact if followed by the long squeal of the laundry cupboard doors. The squeal meant that my mother, unable to sleep, was counting sheets, laundry list in hand. This reading was neither sedition nor entertainment. No matter how many times my mother counted, the laundry list refused to tally. Between one cupboard and the next, counting and re-counting, her footsteps were slow. She sighed. Sometimes she cried. I never went down. You don't disturb people when they're reading.

12

LOVE LESSONS

THE 1967 SUMMER of Love didn't entirely pass us by. Even in northeast Lancashire something wafted over from California. Our nurserymaids' skirts got shorter, their hair longer. They could recognise songs from *Sergeant Pepper*. Pop songs were often about love but it wasn't the kind of love imparted by the nuns at our primary school convent. Our nuns were strictly God's love people.

God's love, we were to understand, wasn't the huggy touchy-feely thing you sometimes found in books. It certainly wasn't the love wafting over from California. God's love was an exasperated kind of love, often involving an improving swish of the cane 'which hurts Him more than it hurts you'. It was terrible imagining God flinching, as we did, under Sister MB's quick flick over the back of the legs or the palms of the hands. Why He didn't break the cane we couldn't imagine. Second Sister managed to crack it with a cleverly concealed pencil-sharpener thus at least once saving God any hurt at all.

Later, at our convent boarding school, we learned that God's love was a transaction. If we wanted to earn more of it we should memorise the catechism, that little book of wisdom which would supply answers to any question a decent Catholic might ask. The questions started encouragingly enough:

Q1. Who made you?

A. God made me.

We knew that God made us to love Him so that we'd eventually make it to Heaven. Complexities arose when love required action. After our night prayers, for instance, we were to 'observe due modesty' and think about death.

'Due modesty' meant you shouldn't look at bodies, not yours, not anybody else's. Nor should you ever acknowledge the existence of those parts or bodily functions about which, according to Sister E, the infirmarian, All Women Should Be Ashamed. Eyes closed in the bath; periods as The Curse brought down on all women by wicked Eve. Brought up as we were, women as contaminants was hardly news. Now, though, we discovered we could atone for our shortcomings by mortifying our bodies – rising at dawn for the nuns' mass; kneeling at night prayers until our knees hurt; not eating a second piece of toast at breakfast. Mortification was a form of love with which I could get to grips. Then a schoolfriend told me that babies were conceived by 'making love'. She knew details. I was staggered. Love? That sounded distinctly slippery slope to me. Not just slippery. A slide. A slide down the slope. A slide right off the end.

'Making love' could at least be put on hold, possibly forever. Not so the love we must show by embracing death whenever God ordained it should arrive. Two questions of immediate and urgent concern. What happened if death arrived whilst I was at boarding school? Would this love include gladly accepting being buried under the laurels with the dead nuns?

The questions weren't fanciful. More than once at the end of boarding school term, as cars rolled up and other girls rolled away, Oldest Sister, Second Sister and I sat on our suitcases, waiting. Even when full of girls, St. Mary's had something sepulchral about it. Empty, it was a mausoleum. We waited and waited. Sometimes my mother had clean forgotten that terms come to an end. Sometimes, dates being a little hazy, she got the wrong day.

'Your father asked if we could keep you until they come south for something else,' Mother B., the headmistress once informed us as the break-up day drew to a close and there we still were. 'I said no,' she continued after a small dramatic pause. 'But your mother has so far to come' (she made that sound our fault) 'you'll have to sleep here at least tonight.'

It seemed only a short hop from sleeping one extra night in a deserted dormitory to sleeping under the laurels forever. 'Please God, don't let me die here,' was always the last item on my long nightly list of requests. More than a request. It was a plea. I made it with what I hoped was the right kind of love. You could never be sure.

13

BROCK, 1967–1978

S URROUNDED BY ROSES and sheltered, protected even, by trees, the dog memorial at the Not-So-Grand house sleeps gently in the garden near the wall that bounds the meadow. Above the stones on which the name of every dog is inscribed, each dog with its own stone, rest two greyhounds, a copy of a marble statue unearthed at Monte Cagnolo – dog mountain – in Italy between 1772 and 1773. Charles Townley, the antiquarian, bought the statue as a lovely and much-loved addition to his fine collection of antiquities. The greyhounds are seated one behind the other, the bitch gently nipping the dog's ear. Together, they're the guardians of a century of Not-So-Grand dog-life, without which our own lives and the life of the Not-So-Grand house would have been so diminished as to be unrecognisable. Naturally, though not always naturally, the best died early and the worst reached a dogged old age. Brock was one of the worst but the way he arrived was the best.

Birthdays were seldom a big thing unless Nanny remembered. Too many of us, I suppose. Our father found it a bore to remember our names, never mind the day on which we made our first and, for us six girls, disappointing appearance. Our mother was better at names. When prompted by Nanny, birthdays could be a big splash with parties and bonfires and splendid teas in the dining room, the whole house en fête. I don't blame my mother for forgetting our birthdays. She probably preferred to forget. For six of the seven of us, childbirth took place at home and though she said, often and loudly, that the old and squeaky gas and air cylinder had long since run out, nobody was listening.

On my ninth birthday I found an envelope on my breakfast plate. The card read 'I am Brock. Please come and fetch me'. Brock turned out to be a rough-haired Jack Russell puppy. Nanny was grim-faced. Not her idea of the perfect present. No matter. My parents had bought him. He was mine.

I say 'bought', though on reflection I don't believe money exchanged hands. Indeed, any money should really have passed the other way. Brock was a monster. In the whole of his life, a much longer life than anybody predicted or, frankly, desired, I think I was the only person who loved that dog, and my love was a complicated swirl of 'I was given him so I must love him' and a romanticized vision of myself and him roaming the moors like a non-tuberculoid Emily Brontë with Keeper. If you take as a measure those he never bit, I'd say Brock himself loved only two people: my mother and Nanny E. Of those two, only Nanny commanded respect, a respect vastly increased when she put his head back together after he picked a fight with an articulated lorry. All of his head, that is, except the eye he left on the tarmac. Even Nanny couldn't do much about that.

Most things in Lancashire are up a hill, so we walked up the hill to fetch Brock from the smallholding on the road that edged the moor. Brock's mother – 'keep yer fingers out of 'er reach' – was tethered a distance away. Also hopeful of snatching a finger were the ferrets, blinking and twittering. The long dogs, lean tails cramped between lean legs, were solely focused on the hens, a depressed crew already resigned to a bloody end.

The puppies were lying in a scrum. With no preamble Brock was hoiked out by his scruff and presented to me. Crouching, I tried to fasten the collar my mother produced from her pocket. Bared puppy teeth nipped no no no. Brock's breeder – I'm using a fancy word for haphazard coupling – was tickled. 'Better wi' a choke chain,' he advised. 'Start as ye mean t' go on.' Brock took this to heart. On the way home there wasn't a sheep, cow, horse, car, van, cyclist, chicken, goose or person not issued with a yapped warning of future persecution.

Nanny forbad Brock the nursery so he mainly inhabited the scullery whose chill never warmed and whose stone floor sweated as though some giant was wetly decomposing beneath.

Roughly a month after he arrived, Brock's yapped warnings heated up. Hot war was declared loudly and indiscriminately on everything that moved. School gerbils brought home for 'safekeeping' were speedily crunched. Ducks in the river were murdered en masse, their carcasses spread about for me to collect and carry to people's doors like some kind of woeful undertaker. Sometimes I had to make two journeys. Major enemies included the postman and the dustmen, the former reduced to throwing the post in the direction of the kitchen window and the latter refusing to touch a bin until 'all clear' had been sounded. Priests were viewed with particular venom. Something about the swish of their black soutanes sent the dog quite berserk. If, to placate, the priests removed their soutanes, in a millisecond their trousers were ripped from top to bottom leaving them hopping about, barelegged. Farmer S., delivering the milk, adopted a more retaliatory strategy. Shaking his milk crate to persuade his persecutor to seize it, he'd lift the crate with the dog attached and crash both against the stone steps.

With non-priestly visitors, Brock sometimes played a longer game. In the drawing room he'd roll over with spaniel sweetness as if wanting to be scratched. In vain did my mother issue warnings. In vain did she exhort people to keep their hands to themselves. In vain did she recite the list of recent victims. Smug smiles said 'don't be so silly! I know dogs!' Perhaps they did. But Brock was a dog only in form. In spirit, he was a demon from a medieval bestiary, all hackles, teeth and damn you to hell.

Eventually, in an attempt to broker peace, Brock was peeled away from the back door and sent to sleep in the attic with me. Despite all evidence to the contrary, I thought we might curl up together.

Early signs were good. He'd settle himself, the low growl almost a lullaby. If I climbed into bed carefully and arranged my limbs artfully, there might even be harmony. But harmony was fragile. The gentlest twitch, the smallest relaxation, and now I was the enemy. First came barked insults, then full-frontal attack – he could draw blood through blankets. Sometimes it was easier to sleep on the floor.

You might have thought all this bad enough, but even greater than his hatred of wheels, dogs, cats, postmen, dustmen and Farmer S., even greater than his implacable hatred of priests, was his hatred of our ponies. Our ponies weren't just enemies, they were outrages, blots on the face of the earth, their presence in the field an unendurable affront. He scowled at them as he went about his daily bloody business and at moments which clearly made sense to him though none to any beholder, he'd erupt through the fence and hurtle towards them. The ponies, heads shooting up, ears shooting back, heels shooting any which way, fled, galloping faster and faster to outpace their small but relentless tormentor.

Why did they never learn? The chase was just a ruse. Brock's real goal was to separate out today's particular victim – if he'd turned his hand to sheep-dogging, he'd have aced – gather himself into a tiny ball, then leap, jaws agape, and with the precise calculation of a laser-guided missile, close his teeth around either a great wodge of tail or, even better, around the tail's bony dock. Whichever, the result was the same. The pony, already demented, would twist and kick, twist and kick as if a mountain lion were on its back. Brock, his body rhythmically battered by two steel-shod hooves, would plunge up and down like the ball on one of those tennis 'come-back' machines. Whack whack whack went the hooves. Up and down, up and down went Brock. When even his iron jaws couldn't clamp any longer, he'd let go, and with a fine dismounting vault, spin up up up before down down down to a crash landing. I would rush over. I can admit it now, as I couldn't then: I did love him, but 'killed in action' seemed a perfectly brilliant end. It never happened. He never was dead. Sometimes he would be half concussed. Often he'd be bleeding. Usually, bits were broken. So I'd carry him home where he'd lie prone, his one eye closed, the empty socket of the other twitching until, ribs still at odd angles and legs still wobbly, he'd heave himself up and go at it all over again.

I wonder now whether, after a particularly harrowing death-spree, with a regretful but liberating sharp stone I could have killed him myself? Had our identities been reversed, he'd not have hesitated to kill me. Yet however despairing I became, whatever tears I shed from pain or frustration, however many corpses I collected, he remained that rare birthday present, proof, though demonic, that my parents had at least once made a plan at which I was the centre. I couldn't have killed that.

So Brock lived on. Only after more than a decade, and when killing him proved beyond anything in the known universe did I help do the deed myself. I can't remember exactly the final straw. My father suddenly announced 'no more' and as Brock's mistress (laughable thought) told me to 'get on with it'. I attached the lead; I put Brock in the car. Getting him into the vet's surgery and through the waiting room without incident was a perilous business. Pet-owners shrank away. The nurse in reception cried 'no further'. The vet demanded a muzzle. This I refused. Brock should depart this life as he entered it: snip snap snip. So, with difficulty, I held him and guided the needle. It wasn't because he bit me that I cried. It wasn't because he fought both me and the vet to the last. It wasn't because a needle death is shockingly quick. I cried because despite the guilty relief, Brock's reign of terror was so embedded in our lives that I knew that we'd never be quite ourselves without him. 'Rest in peace' we intoned over his grave. Anything he'd have liked less it would be hard to imagine.

14

TICKING BOXES

NONE OF THE clocks in the Not-So-Grand house displayed the same time. For accuracy somebody had to go into the flower room to ring the speaking clock's Jane, then after 1963, Pat. We grew on warm terms with the automated ladies although even in the height of summer the flower room – a long, thin room specifically for, yes, arranging flowers – wasn't warm. I suspect my father chose to put the telephone in the flower room to discourage anybody lingering even one second longer than necessary.

I needed no discouragement. I wasn't fond of the telephone. After Brock's arrival its main function was ringing vets, doctors and issuing apologies to the outraged and the injured. In that respect, being Brock-free, the speaking clock was a relief. Also, unlike so much of the Not-So-Grand house's domestic paraphernalia, it was reliable. It was also expensive, but despite the expense, nobody ever suggested that perhaps one clock should tell the right time. In the Not-So-Grand house time was much less important than timing. If you were going anywhere with my father, for example, it was vital to arrive in the hall, ready to go, before he did. If you arrived in the hall after him, no matter what time he'd set for leaving, you were late. Like homicide, regicide, infanticide, fratricide, patricide and matricide, being late was a sin calling to heaven for vengeance.

For my mother, being punctual for hunting mattered; our arrival and departure from school didn't matter. Being punctual for some meetings mattered; for others it mattered so little I'm surprised she got there before the meeting ended. Being punctual for Mass in the house mattered; for Mass elsewhere, there was 'on time enough'. Anything to do with animals, even Brock, mattered. Anything to do with people mattered less. Celebrations, including greeting the New Year, must take their chance. It was years before she realised that her watch no longer worked.

When we were just ourselves, no visitors, we ate in what we called the schoolroom even though it had never seen a lesson. In the schoolroom, the brown wooden-cased clock ran slow. Nobody knew if it was actually slow. We believed it to be slow and in a Catholic household belief is all. 'It's slow,' somebody would say every day, and we'd nod, yes, slow. Once a week my father climbed a ladder and groped about for the large key which lived on the top of the slow clock's clock-case. Key located, he wound, the cogs grinding against each other like an old man grinding his teeth. You expected the clock to spit. My father entrusted nobody else with the task of winding this reliably unreliable grindy clock. As he aged, his ascent and descent on the ladder more perilous, his spurning of help became more vehement. With his typical luck, time was on his side. He never fell, and the clock ticked away 'neither use nor ornament', as Nanny said. All those hours my father spent up the ladder were an absolute waste of time.

Equally unequal to its time-keeping role, the drawing room clock was at least ornament. Freighted with gold, studded with jewels, it was a drama of a thing carried on the back of a black elephant, trunk up, head twisted, startled by and not altogether pleased with, its burden. On top of the clock perched an oriental figure, a large leaf on a thick stalk held aloft as protection from the sun – a little joke in Lancashire. For all its bulk, the clock's chimes were light and musical, not elephantine at all. The last time I saw my mother at home she was in the drawing room wearing a quilted dressing-gown of Venetian red. Determinedly upright in an upright chair despite the cancer that was killing her, she was staring at that elephant and holding on to time, whether accurate or not, for dear life.

The elephant clock hailed, I think, from Zanzibar; my great-grandmother's first husband, Gerald Portal, had been Consul-General there in the late nineteenth century. Time had reduced him to a name pasted onto a hefty sea-going trunk buried in the boxroom. There he sat amongst the mountain of other rejects both large and small that my mother occasionally and despairingly 'sorted', really just pushed about so at least the geography was new.

I passed Gerald Portal's trunk often before I began to think of him as a flesh-and-blood man, a brave man, a brilliant diplomat mourned by the whole British establishment when cut down by typhoid at the age of 35. Ending up as a trunk seemed happier than ending up as one of the attic's ancestral portraits, unhung because nobody cared enough about the sitter to award him or her a space in the light. The unhung were gloomy. Dead Gerald's trunk may have been leaden (I think a man who's now a trunk may be addressed by his first name), even slightly mouldy, but it was far from gloomy. Once you noticed the strapmarks, the remains of handwritten labels bearing the names of faraway places and the dents from rough handling or sea-storms, you couldn't help wondering about the trunk's journeys in ships' holds and on the backs of horses or camels before it was finally carried up the boxroom stairs and dumped, an unglamorous final resting place for a stalwart witness to a glamorous life.

Occasionally, imaginatively speaking, I filled the trunk with Gerald's most intimate accoutrements: his linen, his shoes, the personal things he didn't like to be without. He'd also have had a dressing case, probably pigskin, with velvety slots for razor, shaving brush, lotions and potions. Maybe that was mouldering here too, kept for sentimental reasons much as you keep the collars of dead dogs. Maybe not. According to my grandmother, Great Granny loved only one man and he was neither her first nor her second husband'[*] (Granny's father) so she may have been happy to ditch the dressing-case. In any event, after his death, and unencumbered by children, it didn't take Great Granny long to launch into her first widowhood of admirers, parties and evenings at the opera. 'She was perfectly happy. I don't know why she married my father,' Granny said. More mysterious vagaries.

Great Granny died in 1950 on a definite date, though unless somebody in the room had a watch, the precise time may have been debateable.

You may feel that for somebody I never met, Great Granny appears surprisingly often in this memoir. You're right. Her appearance isn't because of Gerald's trunk, nor even as the root of 'no more slippage'. I think of her often, and hence she appears often, because, apart from my mother, she was the person my father loved best in the world. If I say that he loved her more than us – at least that's how it seemed – this is observation not complaint. We were people he knew, to whom he was vaguely connected. Great Granny was the bedrock of his life. You could feel it. She was the only person of whom he spoke with love, and always with joy. 'This is how she took this corner,' he liked to report as he sped down the lane that linked the Not-So-Grand house with the main road. 'And when she got to the bottom, she looked neither right nor left, just launched smartly out.' We were approaching the bottom of the lane, the main road lying in wait, my father speeding up for the best bit of a story that never palled. 'One day I suggested she might stop and check for oncoming cars and she said "Have you never heard of a little thing called radio location? Everybody knows I'm coming."' He pressed the accelerator. 'Radio location!' he cried gaily as he swept out. My great-grandmother never hit a thing. Nor did my father. There may have been something in radio location after all.

Often, he dropped into conversation other little snippets, just

<hr>

[*] Norman, Priscilla, 1982, In The Way of Understanding, Foxbury Press p8

dribs and drabs in no particular order. I thought at first he was passing Great Granny on – lest we forget as it were. Now I think it was nothing to do with us at all. Rather, it was his way of keeping her with him: a not-letting-go. Sometimes I confused events, not being sure, for example, how much time passed between Gerald's death and Great Granny's second marriage to my great-grandfather, Colonel Robert Reyntiens. My father would look sadly peeved before brightening. 'My grandfather had a mad stepfather, Monsieur de Brouckère,' he said, 'whom my grandmother believed was possessed by the devil.'

'Perhaps this made her Catholicism even more fervent,' I once remarked.

My father was scathing. 'My grandmother's Catholicism wasn't 'fervent' as you call it. It was perfectly normal.'

I wasn't sure how 'normal' it was to send her daughter, my grandmother, aged about seven to sink to her knees in front of the mad Monsieur Brouckère and beg his forgiveness for sins unspecified. According to Great Granny, the old man leapt up shrieking as though Granny had poked him with a pitchfork.

Then my father mellowed. 'When my grandmother died, James [Great Granny's butler] summoned the bishop. When the bishop saw that James had laid her out, head to the altar, a position only allowed for senior members of the clergy, he tried to suggest a change. James was having none of it. "Her Ladyship will remain just as she is." So that's what happened.' I'm not sure why this anecdote afforded my father such pleasure. Perhaps he was hoping for the same head-to-the-altar treatment for himself.

My father didn't find it odd that, unlike Gerald, there was nothing of Robert Reyntiens in the boxroom of the Not-So-Grand house. With the same lack of curiosity he showed about Alice O'Hagan, he'd never asked. He was surprised when I did. 'My grandfather died in 1913, the worst time possible,' my father said, as though this was somehow Robert Reyntiens' fault. He [my father] was more concerned that once war was declared, my great-grandmother and my grandmother, labelled Belgian, had had to register weekly at the police station. A cracking insult, as my father, and I dare say my great-grandmother, saw it, for the daughter and granddaughter of the 7th Earl of Abingdon.

We could never persuade my father to get rid of the impossible wooden bed in which his grandmother died. It was an inconvenient bed needing two people to change sheets specially spun for a specially made mattress specially filled with something specially heavy. Hideously uncomfortable it may have been, but I do understand why he couldn't let it go because I also have an impossible inconvenience. Mine is my Abingdon Great-×-2 grandfather's travelling writing box. Labelled 'portable' yet so heavy it will likely give you a hernia, it's a square affair with the earl's coronet engraved on the top. It may have been on this 'portable' inconvenience that the earl composed the following letter:

Wytham Abbey [the family seat of the Earls of Abingdon], Oxford   May 1889

My dear Joey [family name for his daughter, my father's grandmother, my great-grandmother, Lady Alice Bertie]
Your letter is characteristic of your consideration for yourself and your want of it for others. I desired Jones to discharge all the servants; on arriving here I find that Rosalie, a servant whom I had left here to wait upon Cecil [my great-grandmother's sister] had not accepted the notice in consequence of your taking upon yourself, without asking me, to write and tell her she was going to Graz - I do not suppose you for a moment consider the expense of travelling servants out and back. Gwen [his second wife, my great-grandmother's stepmother] contents herself with what she can find out there - I suppose it seems quite natural to you that she and Cecil should share a maid while you have one to yourself. I think she is about the only person who would have put up with such a thing . . .'

He moves on to her marriage.

'The necessary arrangements will be made for you and I must express my surprise that as it is owing to the date at which you wish to be married we are all put to inconvenience, you should be the person to find fault and show temper – I may also remind you that since your engagement to Grey [Gerald Portal] your behaviour to me has not been such as to entitle you to much consideration. You appear to think that our mission in life is to minister to your fancies – I am heartily sick of your airs and tempers and if you cannot behave yourself during the short time you have to be at home, you may find your marriage arranged for a time and place that suits my convenience irrespective of yours.

I am quite determined not to be bounced by you any longer . . .

Your Affc.

A [short for Abingdon]

[PS] I have nothing to do with your arrangements after your marriage, but when you pay for your own clothes you will probably modify your ideas: if not I fear it will be very disastrous.'

Great Granny's marriage notice reads 'there being no reception . . .' so perhaps her wedding was in the end arranged at a time inconvenient to her. Whatever, my great-grandmother kept this letter and we can't know whether we, her descendants, were meant to laugh or be outraged on her behalf.

We have a photograph of 'airs and tempers' Great Granny with my 'no more slippage' father aged roughly two sitting on her knee, her outraged and inconvenienced father sitting opposite and her 'my living husband is dead' daughter standing behind. My father is gazing at what I think is a pocket-watch held up for his amusement. What a lovely picture of four generations, people say. Indeed, but

as a record of how things really stood between them all, it's about
as reliable as the Not-So-Grand house clocks.

15

STAYING ALIVE

BETWEEN THE AGES of seven and fifteen, my fear for Christmas was that I'd never see it. I wasn't ill or anything like that; I just believed that I might die on Christmas Eve. I didn't worry that my death might wreck anybody else's Christmas. My fear was entirely selfish: I couldn't bear the thought of missing Christmas when I'd spent so many months looking forward to it. Waiting for Christmas was big because Christmas was big. Unlike birthdays or collecting us from school, Christmas was never forgotten, never glossed over, never diminished. Traces of every Christmas celebrated in the Not-So-Grand house still remain – pine needles, nut shells, strands of tinsel, wrapping paper shredded by mice, slivers of food stolen, hidden then forgotten by dogs. The Not-So-Grand house Christmas, always the same, with differences.

The differences stick out, particularly the year our stockings bulged with detritus from the boxroom: wooden rosaries with beads big as golf balls; enamelled boxes just broad enough for pony and dog teeth; lace gloves useless to us; a few of those stubby candles 'with one hour left to burn'. 'We're poor now,' I thought as I pulled out scent testers my mother must have found in a drawer. It didn't matter. The girls in *Little Women* were poor, and Beth, drawing her last breath 'on the bosom where she had drawn her first' was to be envied. Except please God don't let me die until Boxing Day.

Or the day after. Boxing Day was a hunting day. (And don't forget I can't die at school.)

My mother believed that Christmas should be home-made. She had an inbred horror of anything shop-bought, particularly marmalade (except Frank Cooper's), ready-made English mustard, and all bread, strictly no exception. She also thought that things bought in shops smacked of the casual and offhand. There should be nothing casual or offhand about Christmas. Proper Christmas demanded proper time and trouble. Over Christmas cards, the rule was unbending. Over Christmas presents, the rule did waver. Even with the wavering, home-made was the real deal.

We constructed our cards at the nursery table under the watchful but not very creative eye of Nanny. Unlike Eldest and Second Sister, I had no talent for it. My mother, whose creative gifts had, before marriage, gained her a place at the Royal College of Art, was both talented and ambitious. She conjured a whole crib out of paper and thin cardboard: ox, ass, baby and all. The sheep had curly fleeces. She charmed angels from old Floris powder boxes, each round face a different character. One Christmas she decided on lino-cuts for cards and drew two or three elaborate designs. Gouge in hand, she rolled up her sleeves. Within thirty seconds blood was pouring from her thumb. My mother gasped. We gasped. The Christmas juggernaut juddered to a halt. Only momentary. My mother swapped black ink for red and by the time Nanny returned with a bandage the juggernaut was juddering on.

Downstairs, the Not-So-Grand house was decorated entirely with the Christmas cards my parents received. Hundreds of them. Official, personal, the considered, the ill-considered and the stuck-on-an-old-list-as-yet-unculled. When we primly pointed out that every single card was shop-bought, my mother scolded. We must forgive the casual off-handedness of others. It was Christmas. People were busy. Oh, so many retorts to make. We made none.

Upstairs in the nursery we emptied the battered box of Christmas decorations and hung anything hangable from any hangable angle. Like a maiden aunt unwillingly strung about with baubles, the nursery rattled and rustled. From somewhere appeared paper-chain stacks, each sticky coloured loop marking off the seconds until the teatime when my father appeared like a wizard bearing the sugar-sprinkled panettone sent by Count and Countess Giustiniani all the way from Venice. I don't remember eating it, only gazing at it. How tall it was, its sugar like snow! How far it had come! How on earth did you spell panettone for the thank-you letter?

My maternal grandparents often came for Christmas. Unlike my paternal grandparents, both my maternal grandparents were clearly alive, and appeared happy in each other's company. In my memory, my grandmother is metaphorically and sometimes actually sepia-coloured. I don't mean she was stuck in the past, only that her gumboots and tweed skirts accentuated a delicate, ethereal beauty that never seemed completely part of the present. My grandfather seemed the solid one. It was always he who drove, slowly it's true, but I never imagine my grandmother behind the wheel. Perhaps she drove too fast for my grandfather's nerves. In my childish memory, probably inaccurate, he fussed over arrangements; she glided serenely on. He imagined disaster; she had faith that all would be well. Had I shared with my grandmother my fear of Christmas dying, she'd have reassured and soon forgotten. My grandfather would have listened and always remembered. I never doubted for one moment that they both loved me.

Though I know her life had been complicated and at times very unhappy, my grandmother's love seemed simple: she simply loved. My grandfather's love was, unsurprisingly for a survivor of the First World War, more complex. In the summer of 1918, aged nineteen, he'd been commissioned into the Coldstream Guards and sent to France. The odds were stacked against him. His older brother, Tom, aged twenty-seven, had died at Neuve Chapelle. His maternal uncle Henry had died on the Somme. Four of his first cousins – all killed in action. Nothing about these in the diary he kept before going 'up the line' himself. Hard not to over-test your courage by imagining yourself at the end of the list. Instead, amongst all the strange juxtapositions of war – the boredom, the crises; the polo-matches and the route-marching; the exotic food including chickens sent from home and no food at all – he marvelled at his luck at being born a Catholic, 'the religion of love and hope and confidence and complete understanding'.

I wish I'd spoken to him about his astonishing faith. But for a child, the most fascinating thing about my grandfather wasn't what he believed, or what he'd experienced, or the friends he'd left behind in France. The most fascinating thing was what he brought home. Beneath a deep groove in his left cheek lodged a small, jagged lump of metal, a fat and irremovable splinter of Mills bomb, the second fragment of which had travelled further and broken his right jaw. For the rest of his life, when my grandfather ate, the Mills bomb fragment clicked a neat accompaniment and the damaged nerves unleashed a torrent of sweat down his cheek. It was mesmerising.

For many mesmerised years I thought the clicking and sweating the end of the story. It wasn't. When his mother, my maternal great-grandmother, heard that my grandfather, her youngest son, had been injured and was unlikely to survive, she shot herself. 'Don't worry,' an aunt told me in reassuring tones decades later. 'She didn't die at once.' I was momentarily appalled. Then I understood. In 1918, even for those with a depressive streak like my great-grand-mother, suicide for Catholics was a mortal sin. My aunt wanted me to know that there had been time to repent. I always wonder if that's how the news of his mother's death had been relayed to my grandfather. 'She's dead, but don't worry, she had time to repent.' Could somebody really have said that? In any event, even for a man who saw the afterlife as a 'huge garden bathed in sunlight and full of flowers and beauty and clearness', learning that news of his injury and presumed death had pushed his mother over the edge must have been a faith-tester.

I don't know if my grandfather thought about his mother at Christmas. I don't know what he thought about her at all. So often you lose your grandparents when you're still tied up in the selfishness of youth. You accept their focus on you as the natural order and forget to turn the focus around. Also, I'm ashamed to say, when my grandfather was old and I could have asked him anything, his unremitting fretting over my mother's well-being drove me mad. I understood, but didn't like, that fretting is an aspect of love. I also understood that his present fretting over my mother was undoubtedly all muddled up with a past as distressing as any past could be. I like to think I'd be more patient now. But what use is that? My maternal grandfather was a good man – 'the goodest man I ever knew' as one of his soldiers wrote after my grandfather's death. He had been tested physically and emotionally in ways known to few. He'd earned his fussiness and fretting.

Unlike friends' houses where the Christmas tree was up and lit by mid-December, the Not-So-Grand house tree kept to my great-grandmother's timetable. Decorate the tree on Christmas Eve. Tree-lights not lit until after Midnight Mass. So there we all were, in the middle of the night before Christmas, completely at the mercy (or so it felt) of a set of frail multi-coloured bulbs linked by frayed electrical cord attached to a tiny plug made in 1904. It's strange that despite how often the bulbs' gossamer-winged guardians, the little creatures who had a bulb each to look after, turned out to be Christmas saboteurs, I thought them benign. Fifth and Sixth sister had no such illusions. Having inspected the creatures closely, they pronounced them demons. I didn't care. Even if the lights failed, Christmas was here and I was still alive.

One Christmas Day a dog wandered up the drive. We found it in the scullery during the post-Christmas Day lunch bustle. The dog wasn't in a good way, so instead of turning it out my mother encouraged it up the back stairs and into the laundry passage. The laundry passage housed the airing-cupboard so once she'd constructed a bed, the dog would be warm. It was a hairy dog, part collie, part something neither distinguished nor distinguishable. No collar. Just a very hairy dog in a very bad way. Bad way or not, I imagined it would live. After all, 'it takes a lot to extinguish life' and here we all were, emanating life, emanating hope, emanating goodwill to all dogs. Though it would neither eat nor drink, the dog did lick its lips. Eventually we left it to sleep. For the dog, things were as good as they could be: alone but not abandoned; lost but found; ill but tended. We shuffled down to the drawing room where my mother's presents were waiting. She always opened hers after lunch, we opened ours before. She opened her presents and made all the right exclamations. Christmas the same, Christmas different.

Later in the afternoon the dog appeared flatter, less substantial. It blinked at my mother. After a moment, she made her way to the flower room. We knew the pattern. The telephone, the vet, the moment before and the moment after. We didn't wail or cry. The dog had been with us only a few hours and even on Christmas Day it takes longer than a few hours to weave into the fabric of a family. But listening to the vet's careful footsteps – he was worried about bringing mud into the house – I could feel my Christmas Eve fear bubble again. My father was wrong. It didn't take much to extinguish life. Christmas Day wasn't yet over and I was already anxious about next year.

16

GIFTS OF SORTS

THE YEAR FOLLOWING my wicked dog Brock's arrival, Second Sister went off to join Oldest Sister at boarding-school, St. Mary's Convent, Ascot, as solidly south of England as we were solidly north. I don't remember missing Second Sister, but I suppose I did at least for a while, if only because until Brock joined me, though I loved the attic I didn't like facing the spiders alone. Spiders or not, I was determined not to follow Second Sister to Ascot and so hatched a plan. I would work hard, pass my 11+ with brilliance and thus earn a free place at the local grammar. My father would save money. I could stay at home. Everyone a winner.

First intimations of miscalculation wafted from my mother. She looked quite blank when I told her of my 11+ triumph. I wasn't yet eleven and she'd never heard of the 11+, or at least never heard that it might mean anything. I think she thought I was showing off. Showing off merited no congratulation. My father's reaction pulled the rug straight out. 'That's good,' he said. 'They don't want stupid girls at St. Mary's.' Jesus! It had never occurred to me that it might be better to fail. On my last night before exile Brock installed himself inside my school trunk and threatened to tear holes in anybody who came near. It took Nanny, tutting over the carefully name-taped handkerchiefs and the weirdly silky 'function dress', to pitch him out. When we left, me sobbing wildly, Brock harried the car wheels all the way down the drive.

I never took to boarding school. I did feel a little more at home when an inmate escaped from nearby Broadmoor, the high security psychiatric hospital. The Not-So-Grand house, too, had its share of disturbed and disturbing visitors. Our favourite lunatic was quite literally that: a man who went a bit doolally when the moon was full. Sometimes he howled. Sometimes he stole things from the garden. Once he pitched a boulder through the drawing room window with such force that it landed all the way over in the fireplace without skimming the floor. At school, should we meet the escapee, the nuns advised engaging him in conversation, asking perhaps about golf. Golf! Wasn't that just like the south of England! I came from the north. If I met the escapee I'd bark 'ger away wi' yer, ye daft booger', something I'd heard shouted often enough at my dog. That, and the hockey-stick with which I couldn't hit a ball, should do it.

By the time a friend had, albeit inadvertently, killed a squirrel with her hockey stick thus showing us all how to do it, things at school were looking up. I still cried at the beginning of every term but by then I understood something important: since you must have a home to suffer it, homesickness is a sort of gift.

And boarding school brought something else. On the long journeys to and from we sang. My mother, relaxed in the car as she seldom was at home, sang too. Round and round we went with 'Kookaburra Sits In The Old Gum Tree' or 'Sumer is Icumen In', chins tucked in for the plunging low note at the end of 'Great Tom Is Cast'. We could be the Von Trapp children, one of us the Mother Abbess. We could be Maria, yodelling like goatherds. We could sing anything we liked. We sang in parts with confident ease. I've no idea how good we were. Who cared. When we sang I was completely happy.

Assuming my parents remembered to collect us, the best singing journey of the year was the journey home from school for the Christmas holidays. We sang for hours, bickering gently over what carols and songs to perfect for one of the immutable traditions of the Not-So-Grand house, the Great Christmas Present Delivery to Long Retired Retainers. The Not-So-Grand house had accumulated quite a number: Mr. C. the retired gardener, and Mrs C. on Mount Lane; James (the butler who laid out my great-grandmother) now living in Blackburn with his sister; Mrs H. who, with her long-dead husband Syl, had farmed the home farm; Mr. H., Mr. C.'s gardener successor, who had shared his worm-eating with my brother; and, in time, Mrs N., in retirement still squat as a bobbin, round as a millwheel, the waist of her pinny never visible, her legs bandy, her ankles trim. The tradition was of course not immutable. Ancient Retainers die. Children grow up and leave. It just seemed immutable because for years it was unchanged.

The deliveries took a whole afternoon and only worked exactly as tradition demanded when my mother drove. The visitees did love seeing us – young children, old age, Christmas. But my mother, still young herself, was more than an afternoon treat. She was a surviving beacon from that familiar world now being bulldozed along with the Victorian town centres. When she walked through the doors of the visitees, faces lit up and we, as part of her, were reflected in the light.

My mother viewed duty as the practical manifestation of love. Duty without love she deemed a hollow, self-regarding exercise. She may have been in a fuss of Christmas busyness. She may have even longed for the day we could drive and she could spend the afternoon wrapping, organising, cooking, checking, shopping. But she loved all the visitees, and once in the car and we were singing, Christmas fuss and Christmas love declared a truce. Now she was one of us.

As we sang, we counted Christmas trees already flashing and twinkling in the shortness of the days. On the dark road to Blackburn, a cross glowed high above a church tower. Descending or perhaps ascending over the town, it appeared to float free as the cross that, so I learned from a Ladybird book, had appeared to the Emperor Constantine. At the sight of that cross's neon radiance a deep bliss set in. I knew that no visit would be rushed, no cup of tea refused, all cake eaten, or, if it had dreaded currants in it, covertly salted away in a pocket already prepared to receive it.

Before tea, and again before we left each house, we sang carols in three or four parts – sometimes traditional, sometimes from Britten's *Ceremony of Carols*, and always, a favourite, Cecil Broadhurst's 'Cowboy Carol'. Those Christmas visits were ostensibly for others but in so many ways, for us, the visitors, they were the richest Christmas gift of all.

Eldest Sister leaving school, so no longer part of the long car journeys, was our first great family loss. She came home from Paris or London or wherever at Christmas. We still all sang together for the visitees but a fracture is a fracture and breeds more fractures. A year or two after that first fracture, my mother finally succumbed to the Christmas busyness that must have nearly killed her, and my father drove us. The visitees were delighted to see him. There was much family estate chat, many memories of long service. The tradition looked the same; it sounded the same; it wasn't the same. Though the Christmas trees still twinkled and the hanging cross still glowed, the car journey was rushed. Our father drank the tea unwillingly. He didn't want to eat the cake. Despite our singing, the visits were stiffer affairs, the difference, I suppose, between the mutual respect between the visitees and my father and the mutual love between the visitees and my mother.

After Second Sister passed her driving test, the Great Christmas Present Delivery mutated again. Now she drove. A year later it was me. Our mother's love remained undimmed but she had passed on the Christmas beacon. In the end we no longer expected her to come. A sense of mourning crept into our counting of the trees, exclaiming over the cross, delivering the presents, drinking the tea, eating the cake and hiding the currants. The visitees began to die. Finally came the Christmas there was nobody left to visit.

No new Christmas tradition was established. Decades have passed with barely a collective note sung. Like so many gifts, that one has never been, could never be, recreated. But there's a gift in the memory.

As for the homesickness, I've never grown out of it. Even now I can feel that desperation to return to the Not-So-Grand house and never leave. It's a big 'letting go' difficulty. I dream of a miracle that allows me to experience my childhood all over again, not rushing through the days as you do when you're young, this time standing quite still. If I could bequeath any child a gift, that's what it would be: at least once a week to stand quite still and simply be. I know that for some children this would be a curse. For other children, it would seem, at the time, a nonsensical gift. Later, much later, it would seem like the best gift in the world.

17

FOR THE BIRDS

I F MUSIC WAS mainly my father's domain, the animals were my mother's. Her childhood had been filled with horses, dogs, cats, stick insects, myna birds, jackdaws and all kinds of livestock collected by brothers, so this seemed logical. Soon after marriage, my mother acquired a sleeve-peke, Pooh-Bah, a breed it's impossible to imagine her choosing so must have been a present. A dog of leonine pretentions, Pooh-Bah one day leapt out of an inch of open car window to attack an alsation on the other side of the road, with inevitable consequences. My first memory of an animal in the Not-So-Grand house isn't Pooh-Bah, it's my father's Shetland sheepdog, the runt of a litter bred by a friend in a Very Grand House at which my father, pre-marriage, was spending the weekend. For reasons of her own, the little bitch adopted my father. Touched by her unsought yet instant devotion, my father named her Carrie and brought her home. Carrie was frightened of everybody apart from my father and, eventually, my mother. We children could never stroke her. My father took this as a sign of the dog's good taste.

Apart from Carrie, Pooh-Bah and Brock, nobody owned the dogs in the Not-So-Grand house. This was part of the trouble. With nobody exclusively in charge, housetraining was spasmodic, the dogs' lives untroubled by concepts like recall or walking nicely on the lead. Indeed, 'walking the dog' was something my father discouraged. To him, dog-walks were an indulgence. Dogs had the garden. Some of the dogs agreed with him. Those that didn't walked themselves, also with inevitable consequences, so since animals were my mother's domain, death became her domain too.

Considering her childhood menagerie, it was lucky for my father that my mother brought to her marriage only her grey Connemara pony, Gypsy, and the untrumpable qualification that she'd learned to ride on a cow named Mrs Chatty. We were sitting at nursery tea the day my mother told us Gypsy had died. I only recall Oldest Sister, Second Sister and myself being there, so I must have been four. With astonishing self-control my mother didn't cry, not in front of Nanny, not in front of us. Yet I think it was the death of Gypsy more than the birth of us children that marked the final end of my mother's own childhood. Now, instead of a pony, my mother had laundry lists and varicose veins. Instead of friends she had an intolerant husband and squabbling staff. Some years after Gypsy's death, in amongst the retinue of dogs, she also had chickens.

It was my father's decision to get the chickens – 'my grandmother always had chickens' – but the actual chicken keeping was handed over to my mother. She couldn't stand them. 'Don't give them names,' she advised, a gleam in her eye. 'It's more difficult to eat "Betty" or "Hoppity".' Luckily we took her advice as once my mother decided that 'everybody should know how to despatch a bird' the chickens found, or were given, their true calling.

Had my mother had a punchbag the chickens might have survived. Absent a punchbag, the chickens were the unlucky proxies for my mother's honeymoon pregnancy, her second pregnancy barely a minute later and the third barely a minute after that; for the different sets of china my father insisted should be used for different meals because for lunch to appear on the breakfast china was The Slippage to End All Slippages; for all that dressing for dinner when as a permanently pregnant woman she never wanted any bloody dinner on any bloody china, she just wanted to go to bed. I also think that had my father witnessed my mother with the chickens, particularly her neck-snap execution technique, he might have despatched the chickens himself. As it was, my father had no quarrel with the chickens so never went near them.

Those beastly chickens. They lived in the chicken pen, a spartan desert boasting roughly two strands of grass a year and whose chief use beyond the chickens was as a starvation paddock for greedy ponies at risk of laminitis. Perhaps it's no wonder there was always something wrong with those birds, something amiss with their joints or wattles or crops or shanks or eyes or feathers or beaks, or their shit was green, or something supposed to be red had turned purple. They didn't lay properly, producing either too many eggs or none at all. The only thing those chickens did successfully was run rings round Mr. D., he of doleful countenance, tasked with shutting them in at night. 'If Mr. D. can't get them in,' Ma told us, 'the foxes may save us a lot of bother.'

The foxes didn't save us. When the day of despatch dawned we trainee executioners were lined up, hearts in boots.

Even with the chickens my mother's sense of what was and what wasn't proper remained unclouded. 'It's important to be neat despatchers,' she instructed. With her customary flight of arbitrary fancy, she thought it helpful to advise taking our lead from Anne Boleyn's French swordsman and not Thomas Cromwell's 'ragged and boocherly' axe-man. According to Cromwell's contemporary Edward Hall, this axe-man 'very ungoodly perfourmed the office'.

'Obviously we're not using sword or axe,' my mother said, 'because when you meet a bird that needs despatching it's unlikely you'll have either of those things to hand.'

In any case, she herself favoured the stretch and snap or, if we preferred, the sharp twist 'as if you're wringing something out'. Key to both was speed, confidence and no gloves. She demonstrated on something, I've forgotten what, except that it wasn't a chicken. We dutifully copied. Stretch/snap. Sharp twist. 'Snappier,' snapped my mother. 'Sharper.' She inspected our technique, making small adjustments. 'Not too sharp or the head will fall off. Heads on.'

We approached the chicken pen. Making entirely the wrong

choice, the chickens scritched scratched up their hut's wooden ramp, a clucking procession of the unwittingly condemned. Both trepidatious and purposeful – the worst possible execution combination – we followed. My mother quietly bolted the door and in less time than it takes to write this, extinguished the life of Chicken One. 'Speed and confidence,' she said. 'Off you go.'

The worst bit turned out to be catching your murderee – flutter flutter FLUTTER; squawk squawk SQUAWK; peck peck PECK; skitter skitter SKITTER – but at least by the time you did get hold, you were at one with my mother in wanting the damn thing dead. There was one decapitation. My mother frowned. 'More careful, please.' I went for the twist method but it's not easy to keep a chicken's body stuffed under your arm when it knows you're trying to wring its neck. Under those feathers, nothing's as it seems. There are fat bits and thin bits and pointy bits and blunt bits, and all the time the chicken's eye is blinking and all the time there's the squawk squawk squawking, flutter flutter fluttering and peck peck pecking. Looking back, for our sake and the chickens', we should have planted a bomb.

The deaths of my Chicken One and Chicken Two were Crom-wellian and I apologised before reverently laying down the corpses. Chicken Three was more Anne Boleyn. No apology. By Chicken Four I'd given up on reverence. Chicken Five was despatched and tossed aside. Soon we were wringing and flinging like my mother. Then suddenly the henhouse was silent. By the door, the piled corpses twitched. 'Nerves,' Ma reassured. 'They'll have stopped by the time we gut them.' Gut them! Christ!

With the dead chickens in sacks and unexpectedly heavy, like a procession of the temporarily reprieved we stumbled down the henhouse ramp into the chicken pen that was no longer a pen for chickens. My mother didn't say 'well done'. I don't think this was because we hadn't done well – the sacks were compelling evidence. It was because death was a serious affair. I don't suppose many axe-men were congratulated.

We laid the corpses out on newspaper in the scullery. We'd killed the chickens. Now we'd pluck the chickens. Then, heart-quail, we'd gut the chickens. Finally, we'd eat the chickens. If the chickens weren't pleasing, the logic was.

I don't remember plucking the chickens, only the gutting. 'Like this,' my mother said, reaching her hand into what was once a chicken and was now just a cavity. Out came a whole bundle of pinkish, reddish even greenish organs. She swiftly identified heart, liver, gizzard and tossed them into the stockpot. 'Watch you don't puncture anything.'

The first time you stick your hand into a chicken's innards, it's like fumbling around in a nightmare Christmas stocking, all sinister shapes and squelchy textures. It also feels faintly rude and there's more in there than you'd think possible. We were tentative. Bits came out. More bits came out that should be attached to other bits. To start with our mother was quite impatient. Then, from one of the chickens appeared a couple of eggs, shells still soft. 'Aaargh!' we cried, and 'eek!' And to my surprise my mother also cried 'aaargh!' and 'eeek!', outbursts I didn't hear from her again until the day I brought two lobsters home. 'Aaargh!' we cried, and 'eeeek!' as we threw them into a pot of boiling water. I reminded her of the chickens as we hid behind the door. 'I haven't been frightened of dead things since those executions,' I said. 'Spooked, yes, because dead things feel so different. Dead weight isn't just about weight, is it. It has a kind of clotted mass. Those chickens were so heavy in the sack.'

Her back to the door, she hazily remembered. 'Those awful chickens. Always something wrong with them. Did we kill them to eat at something – a party?'

'No, I think we just killed them. It was three of us children and you.'

'We killed them all at once?'

Now I was disconcerted. How couldn't she recall something so big, so seminal, so utterly memorable? It wasn't until my own children grew up that I realised that when parents do strange things with their children, they (the parents) are usually thinking about something quite else: present and absent at the same time. 'Well,' I said, 'that's what I remember.'

She nodded slowly, whether accepting my memory or because her own was returning I don't know. We went back into the kitchen. She poked the lobsters. 'Dead,' she confirmed, and popped the lid back on. We stood as the lobsters cooked. 'I do hate chickens,' my mother said after a while. 'Still, what a peculiar thing to do.'

18

ONE PERFECT DAY

Y OU CAN ONLY have a perfect day in retrospect. You can't plan one. Even if we pretend they don't, planned perfect days always disappoint. For perfection, you need something unexpected. It's the unexpectedness you remember. It's the unexpectedness that clinches perfection.

I don't know when my day started to be perfect. Certainly not in the morning. Bits of the Not-So-Grand house kitchen had collapsed. Without a kitchen, most houses are at sixes and sevens and the Not-So-Grand house was no exception. I don't like sixes and sevens now and I didn't then. In my recollection Nanny is also absent. Disruption in the kitchen and absent Nanny. This day wasn't just sixes and sevens, it was a minefield, our father in a temper because having workmen in the kitchen was irredeemably slippery slope; our mother, tired, pregnant, edgy, wanting to be somewhere, anywhere, else; siblings in squabblesome mood. Everything the wrong way out.

The only glimmer of hope was the sun which rose golden in the morning and settled boldly into the china-blue sky. In north-east Lancashire, even bold sun retreated at the slightest hint of opposition. You couldn't rely on it. Anyway, sunshine alone doesn't make a perfect day although in summer, and this was summer, it's difficult to imagine a perfect day without it.

A glimmer of possibility arrived with my father's departure, taking with him the threat of volcanic blasts over how he, a stickler for mealtime formality, could be expected to survive even a day with no food from the kitchen, no table on which to put any food from elsewhere, and no chairs. Though we children had splendid picnics with my mother in remote wildernesses away from home, eating a picnic in the Not-So-Grand house's garden was considered suicidally slippery slope. The merest hint cast a shadow over even the most blazing sun. No matter now, as off he went. I'm not sure how I knew he wouldn't return that day, I just did, and though tempers were still precariously balanced, my mother's jagged edges immediately smoothed. Food, she knew, was important, but it no longer mattered what we ate or how we ate it.

We all trooped outside. I think we played for a while, possibly still squabbling, but as pale summer warmth deepened into a rare velvety heat, the bickering smudged and a delicious languor descended. The broad steps outside the drawing room windows, usually forbidden to us, were perfect for lounging. We lounged. My mother brought out sun hats usually only worn abroad. Seduced by the heat, she sat down and lounged herself, such an unusual sight that for some time I didn't dare blink in case she vanished. The sun continued to shine. We dozed or got lost in books. Not much talking. A tray appeared – my mother must have found lunch from somewhere. I can't remember what we ate only that we ate with our fingers. Then just the beautiful nothingness of a beautiful day in a beautiful garden, the shushing of the trees (always wind), the occasional judder of a goods-train on the line over the field, the occasional childish yelp at a buzzy insect and my mother, unpinned, undisturbed, completely with us.

You can list the physically perfect elements of a day, and when you're young you feel they are the perfection. They aren't. The beautiful nothingness, the shushing trees, the juddering train, the buzzy insects and the presence of my mother, quiet, serene, unharassed, were aspects of perfection. But the actual perfection, the solid, unshakeable sense of perfection, the reason why I remember that day, was the unexpected feeling of untouchability, of security.

This wasn't physical security. Nanny was absent, Sunday would bring the Prayer for the Queen with the threat of enemies to be vanquished, and I was a non-inheriting girl. But still. This was my home. I knew it. I felt it. Whatever happened, I would know it and feel it. Nobody could take that knowing and feeling away.

At tea-time, my mother stirred. From somewhere, she brought out cake. The cake was sticky and into this tea-time stickiness slimed a slug. It was a large slug, its mantle slightly pinkish, its skirt ridged black, its tentacles aloft. 'It wants cake,' said my mother, and carefully placed a wedge, almost a piece, on a flat stone. The slug slimed towards the cake, seemed to inspect it, then very slowly curled its whole self around the whole wedge. In less than a minute there was only the slug on the stone. My mother offered more cake. The slug curled and ate. She offered more again, this time with a gob of icing. Now the slug didn't bother curling. It just opened its fishy mouth and slurped up the cake with its sluggy undulating gums. 'If we carry on feeding it,' my mother said, 'it will probably explode.' Her eyes were twinkly. The slug was greedy. Perfect days can have perfectly revolting endings.

19

SEWING POTATOES

S O FAR AS I know we didn't have a big sign at the bottom of the drive of the Not-So-Grand house saying 'dump your horse here', so I'm not sure how we became popular repositories for other people's discards, those 'get rid quicks' slyly packaged as 'would you likes', plus the surpluses that accumulate because children grow and ponies don't. One discard arrived with an apology: his rider's 'electric bottom' sent the horse crazy. Our bottoms weren't plugged into the grid, and anyway, our mother never looked gift horses in the mouth. When presented with Mr. Crazy, Second Sister and I took one precaution. He had a startlingly long and unkempt mane and an untamed tail so we took a punt that what had succeeded, up to a point, for Delilah with Samson, might succeed, up to a point, for us. Pulling Mr. Crazy's mane and pulling and trimming his tail was a full day's work but blow me down, for once the Bible wasn't fibbing. It's true that what emerged from the hair wasn't Samson. What emerged was God if God was clever and willing and jumped anything you aimed at.

The only test to which we never subjected Mr. No-Longer-Crazy was the pony trap. We weren't really a 'pony and trap' family but like her grandfather who, when he wanted to harness up, took whatever horse was closest, usually a failed racehorse, and shrugged off disasters because life was a dangerous business, my mother liked a challenge. Our yard of discards didn't include failed racehorses.

Instead my mother eyed up the ex-police-horse, the unbroken two-year-old, the stalwart cob, the flighty thoroughbred, anything that could be persuaded to reverse between the shafts. 'You never know till you try,' she exclaimed brightly as the experimental pony skittered about, the trap bumping and swaying, and us bumping and swaying on the driver's bench. 'Off we go!' And off we went, sometimes rather quicker, sometimes rather slower than expected. 'Everybody should be able to harness and drive a pony,' my mother declared, and in keeping with the bare-handed killing of chickens, 'you never know when it might be needed.'

I'm trying to remember the first time I was conscious of my mother as a rider or, more accurately, a horsewoman. It may have been seeing her on the lane aboard a smart half-bred bay cob, a wide white stripe down his face, a spring in his step. It's a vivid memory. I was in a car. Even through the car window my mother's delight was palpable. Though clearly a little nervous, she shone. The horse was Cheeky. He didn't last long, not because he bit my brother's head – 'I expect he thought you were an apple'. Another baby loomed. Cheeky was sold and a few years later fell victim to an outbreak of lethal horse-slashing. His picture was in the newspaper. I couldn't read the report.

I did, though, through that car window, begin to catch a glimmer that riding wasn't something my mother did – she went riding – it was something she was: she was a rider. Going riding is a temporary pleasure. If you're a rider you're a rider whether you're on a horse or not. And my mother was more than a rider: she was a horsewoman, with a horsewoman's instincts and skills. I don't mean she was one of those horsey women so beloved of cartoonists. Far from that. As true musicians have a musical understanding beyond instrumental technique, so my mother had a poetic understanding of horses beyond the practicalities of feeding, tacking up and staying in the saddle. She never spoke about herself in poetic terms, but when she died and her obituary read 'Mary Towneley, horsewoman' she would have known it to be true.

Before Mr. Crazy, or indeed any pony, arrived, and still too young to know if we'd ever be horsewomen, we had lessons. Dressed like cutouts from a 1930s photograph, we passed our one riding hat between us like the eye between the Graeae sisters of mythology, as though falling off ran to a schedule. Between lessons we immersed ourselves in our mother's childhood pony books – *A Pony for Jean; Another Pony for Jean.* Jean was so lucky! One pony would do us! And then, suddenly, here was a pretty little Exmoor mare, bright bay with the sweetest mealy nose. 'She's yours,' said our mother. Our happiness was unconfined.

Only momentarily. Within an hour, possibly a minute, it was clear that Miss Pretty's notion of happiness and ours were unmatched in every respect. We wanted to catch her; she didn't want to be caught. We wanted to ride; she didn't want to be ridden. We wanted to stay on; she wanted us off. Picking ourselves up after she ditched us, we wanted to re-catch her; she didn't want to be re-caught. All in all, riding for two bronco minutes took all day and quite often ended up in A and E. 'Horse or dog' the nurses asked, barely looking up. With us, it was always one or the other. 'Offer all suffering up for the Holy Souls in Purgatory,' urged the nuns at school. By the time Miss Pretty had been with us a month, there can barely have been a Holy Soul left to save.

You can feel quite near to death when catapulted from even a small pony. Death was, of course, frightening. More frightening, though, was the prospect of incapacitating injury which, after the immediate flurry of attention, would tail off into exasperation, then boredom, then nothing at all. Hard to forget Miss L. on the top farm who'd been discovered dead in her chair by the 'man from the Pru' when he came to fetch the weekly money. She'd been dead a while. 'We wasn't speakin',' said Miss L.'s brother by way of explanation. At the Not-So-Grand house we had no visits from the man from the Pru. If I died in the attic and Nanny also forgot, my corpse might be there still.

A reprieve arrived in the shape of a piebald with a short-fuse temper, a wall eye, a crib-biting habit and a Houdini escape-itch. He also kicked so in company he wore the red ribbon of shame. Didn't matter. He preferred us on than off. The threat of death receded for me; Second Sister bravely stuck with Miss Pretty. The Kicker came for a summer and stayed until he died over twenty-five years later, mostly with his ears flat back.

With the Kicker installed, and once Second Sister and Miss Pretty had negotiated a ceasefire, the moor beckoned. We liked to go fast, so fast we went over scar and scarp, swamp and sedge, granite and moss, steep up, steep down, searching out the sheep-tracks sometimes visible sometimes invisible. With an Exmoor's instincts for the less lethal path, Miss Pretty skipped through bogs and over tussocks with the Kicker slithering and sliding in her wake.

Now I felt something of the shining delight I'd seen emanating from my mother through the car window. More than delight. The treacherous ground generated a particular kind of faith: us in our ponies; our ponies in us. All riders will recognise the special delight in that.

The moors aren't chatting terrain – the wind blows every word away. Instead, our ears tuned themselves into the muted scuffle of hooves on rush and reed, the occasional grind of steel shoe against loose stone, the larks, the curlews, and the rattle of runoff barrelling down the cloughs. Occasionally we stopped to catch our breath. If the rain let up, on one side or other, sometimes both, a distant reservoir gleamed silver and grey.

There was a fullness to this riding, and despite the ceaseless shifts in colour and texture, a stillness. Who wanted to be Jean with the Countless Ponies when we had Miss Pretty and the Kicker, a horsewoman for a mother and a world of our own to which Jean could never belong?

Children are fickle. Down from the moor, the ponies back in the field and the fullness fading, we decided that Jean did have something we wanted. She looked smart and went to shows. We'd like to look smart and go to shows too. We asked our mother. She raised an eyebrow, then agreed.

Thus a self-inflicted agony. Unlike Jean, we were not allowed to plait our ponies' manes the night before a show. 'They'll rub their manes off and be bald' was the reason given, a fiction too alarming to test. So we had to plait on the show day, and that day was, inevitably, a Sunday. Easier to face a firing squad than be late for Mass. Women might be spiritual contaminants, but where Mass in the Not-So-Grand house was concerned, we were contaminants who must on no account be late.

Our first problem with plaiting was size and scale. Long as we might for the thin silky manes and tails of neat little thoroughbreds, Miss Pretty and the Kicker were common creatures with manes thick as hedges and about as accommodating. Tails, similar. And the Kicker kicked.

Our Sunday plaiting theory was sound. Set two alarm clocks for 4.30 am. Have ready two buckets, first for washing, then to stand on – easier to plait from above – button thread cut to length (elastic bands were another on the Absolutely Forbidden list); several darning needles (you always lost at least two somewhere in the hedges of mane); scissors; a mane comb. You were supposed to divide the mane into neat, evenly sized, controllable little bunches. My bunches were fat, uneven absconders. Sometimes I forgot that the Kicker's mane grew on two sides so I'd only plaited half a plait. With a whole plait I could never get the thread tight enough to hold the bottom together. The ponies got bored. The plaits bounced apart. And tick tick tick went the clock, the louder the tick, the clumsier my fingers. Any plaits that were secured looked like potatoes. Jean's plaits, we could absolutely bet, never looked like potatoes.

What had we been thinking? We had the moors! Who needed smartness and shows? Too late now for regrets. Onwards, onwards. At 5 a.m. Mass seemed a lifetime away. I could thread my needle without my hands shaking. By 7.30 I could barely see the needle. More haste, less speed Nanny would have said. But the stables weren't Nanny's domain, so more and more haste, less and less speed. By 7.45 my heart was hammering. At 8.20, crisis. The plaits weren't finished and the ponies' tails still floated free. At 8.25, my father's car crash-crunched up the stable drive, the noise a reasonable indicator of his state of mind. That was it. We perched, paralysed, on our buckets.

My father got out of his car. Some men would have shouted. He didn't shout. Most of his rage flowed into his hands which shook with the force of a delirium. So there he stood, leaning slightly forward, his hands shaking, and there we stood, still on our buckets, paralysed except for our hands, which shook in sympathy with his. Silent, and in my memory rain is now falling, we spat out our needles, posted our ponies into the stables and crept home. Past a wall of disapproval, we sidled into the drawing room, the oratory curtain already drawn back, Mass underway. Despite both epistle and gospel urging patience and forgiveness, my father 'nursed his wrath to keep it warm'. When his wrath was finally unleashed it was very warm indeed.

Yet it's strange. My sharpest recollection of show days isn't the awful potato plaiting or my father's wrath. Nor is it the disappointment of learning that effort and success are in no way related (we usually returned rosette-less). It's not even that despite what people tell you, the joy of taking part seldom compensates for the misery of failure. It turns out that my sharpest recollection of show days is nothing to do with any of that at all. Rather, it's the shame, the unutterable shame, of arriving at the show field in a borrowed trailer emblazoned with the legend 'Premium White Boars'. Even Jean would never have got over that.

20

UNSETTLING RECORDS

THE WORST SIGHT in the Not-So-Grand house world. Not a show day, but inevitably a Sunday. Mass had just started, and there they were, Miss Pretty and the Kicker, escaped from their field, wandering nonchalantly down my father's precious lawn. If only we hadn't looked out of the window! Now we couldn't look anywhere else. My mother pulled her mantilla over her eyes and pretended she hadn't seen. My father, still unaware, was blithely skipping through the Confiteor: '*ideo precor beatam Mariam semper Virginem, beatum Michaelem Archangelum, beatum Ioannem Baptistam . . .*'. Any moment now the movement outside would catch his eye then three things would happen; first, a sharp intake of breath; second, a glare of such startling fury as to stop your heart; thirdly, Mass, already speedy, would beat the current record of seventeen minutes start to finish.

Our early teenage Mass slouch abandoned, we knelt bolt upright, praying, pleading for God to 'DO SOMETHING'. Meanwhile the ponies, sensing perhaps that they'd been spotted, seamlessly swapped leisurely tourist for enthusiastic explorer. At the saunter, even though the grass was wet, not too much damage. At a lively canter, clods of lawn span as from eight mini excavators. The ponies swerved from lawn into beds. Flowers were chopped, shrubs squashed, bushes shredded. 'Carnage' Second Sister muttered. In gardening terms it was.

His back to the windows, our father was, miraculously, still oblivious. '*Credo in unum Deum,*' began the priest. My father took it up, '*Patrem omnipotentem, factorem coeli et terrae, visibilium omnium et invisibilium*'. A shadow, a something, and my father turned his head. No more *invisibilium*.

Oh God Oh God.

As predicted, Mass accelerated. The priest, puzzled and none too pleased, tried to slow the pace. The Consecration must observe due propriety, surely. '*Qui pridie quam pateretur, accepit panem in sanctas ac venerabilis manus suas . . . Per omnia . . .*'

My father's Amen cut off the rest. The Pater Noster was a sprint, the Agnus Dei a full-on charge, we were rushed to communion like the Gadarene swine to the cliff-edge. Only after '*Ite, Missa est*' was there a slight waver because as you'll remember, after the dismissal we had to pray for the queen, and whilst God could be rushed, there could be no rush for her, not for ponies, not for fire, not even for a precious garden.

Priest: 'Oh Lord, save Elizabeth our queen.'

Us speaking slow slow slow to put off the awful moment of reckoning: 'And hear us on the day we call upon Thee.'

Priest, glancing up. Everything quick quick quick and now slow slow slow? Were we taking the piss? (In his head, he may have used more respectable language.) 'Almighty God, we pray for Thy servant, Elizabeth, our queen, now by Thy mercy reigning over us. Adorn her more with every virtue and remove all evil from her path . . .'

And now, just for a second, ponies forgotten, waiting for the phrase of doom 'and vanquish her enemies'. Passed over! No obliteration this week! Onwards, then, to 'that with her consort and all the royal family she may come in grace to Thee who art the way, the truth and the life. Through Christ Our Lord'. 'Amen' I shrilled, the small relief of nuclear survival smothered beneath the terror of imminent human detonation.

Conscious at last that some calamity must be upon us, and nervous lest his breakfast be interrupted, the priest hurried along behind my father's brisk clip from the drawing room to the hall where, abandoned with no explanation, he struggled with the vestments alone. My father returned to the drawing room at a run, his fury shooting us out of our seats like a blast from a fireman's hose. Still in Mass clothes, no time even to change shoes, we tumbled through the garden door shrieking at the vagabond ponies. Excited by our excitement, they ricocheted back to the lawn to perform some fancy dressage for the benefit of my father, stamping each hoof deliberately in turn, tails high for maximum disrespect.

Like elderly ladies zealously collecting for the NSPCC we shook buckets of bribery-food. The ponies' interest was trifling. Who wanted nuts when tree peonies, old-fashioned roses, geraniums and spiraeas were on offer? And what was in the bottom garden, the one beyond the wall? They cantered off to find out. We glanced back to the house. Our father had disappeared. Now we knew visceral fear.

Upstairs was the .22 rifle he kept loaded and ready to despatch rabbits from his dressing-room window. Any minute now we'd see the rifle's single barrel poking out, shifting this way and that like the muzzle of a tank. He usually missed the rabbits but ponies were bigger than rabbits. He might actually hit one. We shook the buckets, shook them and shook them. 'He'll kill you, he'll kill you!' we sobbed. 'Or perhaps he'll kill us!' What cared the ponies?

Round and round galloped the two buccaneers. We vainly charged after them, calling and calling until our voices were drained of all power and urgency. Like mechanical toys running out of battery, our bucket-shaking collapsed into the occasional and desolate. Breakfast time came and went.

Abject despair set in for us at about the same time as boredom for the ponies. Gardens weren't as much fun as they thought. The grass was short; the flowers tasteless. With us dribbling along behind them, it wasn't a peaceful day out. One looked at the other, and with the equivalent of a shrug and a last cheeky huzzah, they cantered up the lawn and trotted back through the escape route gate. In moments their heads were down, grazing resumed. Panting, we rushed to shut the gate. We shot its good solid bolt. The Kicker looked up, working his jaws. Bolt, sholt, dolt: if he wanted out, he'd be out. He lowered his head and forgot about us.

Down the wrecked lawn we shuffled, gloomily facing a day with sand and spades digging in the divots, our father's imprecations ringing louder in our ears than our mother's more sympathetic 'let them have breakfast first'. We collected what we needed and huddled down, silent and, so far as we could manage, out of sight. Fifteen minutes, start to finish, a new Mass record, we said to cheer ourselves up as we dug, patted and smoothed, dug, patted and smoothed. How had two ponies made so much mess?

Later, gazing out of the nursery window, I wondered why, when I wanted so badly for everything to go right, even at Mass everything could go wrong. Life seemed shouty and unfair, and with my own small kick of resentment a traitorous question sprouted: if Mass only took fifteen minutes, what was the point of going at all? I squashed the question. Our ancestors had died for the privilege of hearing Mass. That was all the answer I should need, and in most ways it was. Nonetheless, the question nudged, and though the garden was now peaceful, the question didn't seem as securely squashed as the divots.

21

TAP DANCING

THERE ARE THINGS in life that fill each individual sense: touch, sight, hearing, smell, taste. Often they're quite ordinary things yet their resonating power isn't ordinary at all. Usually, it's just the one sense that returns you to something or something to you: the scuff of velvet to my portrait dress; periwinkle blue to my Grandmama's eyes; the jigger of a pulley to the laundry passage; pizza to Rosa. There are a few places, though, which fill every sense. Sometimes those places are big and grand: the opera house, the vaulted cathedral, the dining room in an old-fashionedly splendid hotel. My every-sense immersive place isn't big or grand. It's the forge to which we rode our ponies once every six weeks to be shod.

Many forges were moveable. Not Mr. C.'s. I don't think he believed in the moveable. His forge reflected himself: static, stone and, to us at least, unchanging because to us he was always in his forge. I couldn't imagine him in a house. In every sense, he was the forge; the forge was him.

We rode the roughly three miles to the forge or, if the pony had lost a shoe, we walked, leading the pony. This wasn't a wild scramble up the moor. Quite the opposite. To get to the forge we rode down the lane and turned left into Burnley. Sedate. Tarmac. Pavements. Heart-sinkers.

One compensation. At the end of a line of stone villas on the outskirts of Burnley a small field hung on, its only inhabitant a

128

skinny horse we named Carmina. We planned one day to rescue her, though from what and to what we never worked out. She disappeared before her field was swallowed up. I don't know why she's still in the back of my mind, one of those images that stick when much more important stuff vanishes.

The forge, though. Iron chimney punched through a corrugated roof, the building itself was a gift to a film director in search of a storybook cottage for a rough-tough urban witch. Why not? Burnley had played a big role in Bryan Forbes's *Whistle Down the Wind* and during the war had been the evacuee home to both the Old Vic and the Sadlers Wells Ballet Company. It was strange to think of Sybil Thorndike and Tyrone Guthrie (director, not actor) asking for cigarettes in cut-glass accents. Impossible to think of Margot Fonteyn having a shampoo and set amid the belch and graft of the mills and the factories. Not that Burnley was unused to incomers. From the start of the twentieth century, Italians fleeing poverty had arrived with only the clothes on their backs and a willingness to get stuck in. Fancy thespians avoiding German bombs may have been rather different, but they were still incomers. When the ballet returned to London, I wonder if any of the dancers ever visited again.

I hope they didn't. In those wartime days, Burnley may have been grubby but it had its Victorian pride. Riding to the forge in the 1970s we ran straight into 'take a club! smash the past!' Burnley. Whether wittingly or unwittingly, the town seemed bent on squandering its pride, the most common sight being the wrecking ball swinging like a malevolent giant eyeball through homes, churches, workhouses, foundries, factories, mills, the old market hall, anything and anybody that looked backwards. This included us. Like Bank Hall pit, Towneleys were the past. To avoid the giant eyeball we hurried along, eyes averted from the Keirby Hotel, opened in 1960, proudly in the vanguard of the architectural monstrosities to come.

Happily, even as Burnley slid from industrial furnace into post-industrial stagnation, Mr. C. held out, hopeful of a return to the days when an invitation to address Burnley's citizens was a significant milestone for any politician or union man. Mr. C., never anything less formal even when we were grown up, had views. He had standards. All Burnley's malevolent eyeball had was wrecking.

Trips to the forge notwithstanding, at the Not-So-Grand house we were protected from Burnley. I don't mean 'protected' in the sense of shielded from, only that it was 'town', thirled to the bottom of the hill and we were country, thirled to the top. There were other separations. Our primary school was part of Burnley and in some ways we were just like all the other children, with siblings in nearly every school form, the gap years a silent revelation of miscarriages or other disasters. We too ate the school lunch gloop. We too longed to be chosen as the May Queen, the epitome of primary school virtue and beauty, or at the very least one of her attendants.

In other ways we were not like the other children. Sometimes in suits, sometimes in overalls, their fathers were people who worked in the mills that survived, or at Lucas's, or Mullards, or Belling or other 'works', or had shoe-shops or other shops, or were profes-sionals – doctors, surgeons, solicitors and suchlike. In other words, unlike our father, these fathers did things you could name. Their kitchens didn't have sheep's heads on the boil. Their nan was their grandmother not their nanny. Most fundamentally, they weren't sent away to boarding school. We accepted the differences, as did they. In north-east Lancashire acceptance was still the watchword of those times.

I wonder if any of my primary school friends knew (as a child I would never have said) that almost better than birthdays was being invited to their house for tea. The invitations were rare and accepted in a flutter of nerves lest something happened and the invitation was withdrawn. When the day came, the relief! First of all, at home-time we went on the bus – oh, the magic of the bus; secondly, friends' mothers never forgot I was coming; and thirdly, for tea we sometimes had sliced white bread and chips in newspaper, delicacies considered so slippery slope in the Not-So-Grand house that they were never even mentioned let alone made an appearance. Half a lifetime later, I still get a chip-thrill and a white-sliced-bread thrill.

Mr. C., a master-craftsman who made his own horseshoes from steel rods stacked above his head, had white-sliced sandwiches for his lunch, or sometimes chips, and drank milky tea syrupy with sugar. Though we were at the forge for hours, we never took lunch ourselves. We never thought of it, not even after the Kicker, for his own lunch, snatched the wreath from a coffin we met at unexpectedly close quarters as we rode down. We found a different kind of lunch, I suppose, a multi-sensory feast of chips, vinegar, thick mugs, white-hot steel, red-hot coals, warm leather, the thump of the wooden toolbox, the soft shearing of the paring knife, the clink of nails. Older horses stood, snuffling, heads drooping. They knew the score. Younger horses shuffled, heads raised, occasionally swishing a tail or stamping an impatient foot.

Sometimes I took my book but it seemed impolite to read whilst Mr. C. was sweating over his labours. Instead, book unopened, I was hypnotised by the rhythm of hammer on anvil (tap TAP tap TAP), the rake-huff-rake of the heating fire, the whoosh of sulphurous steam as hot shoe met cold hoof, and the hiss of the cooling trough.

With the shoe deemed perfect, Mr. C. would pause to mop his brow. Then followed hammer on nail (tap tap TAP, tap tap TAP, tap tap TAP) and the grind of the rasp (rsssh, rssssh, rssssh), and humming through it all, Mr. C.'s gentle crooning, 'there now, coom up, coom on tatie' or 'coom on tatie-face'. The ponies loved that crooning. They'd listen, one ear back, half-hypnotised themselves as each shoe was fitted and secured. Like all good farriers Mr. C. was light on his feet but everything in the forge was heavy: tools, people, air. We sank into it. The ponies sank into it. I never saw an animal Mr. C. couldn't croon into torpor.

When every clench was rasped flat, every hoof back on the floor and everybody had sneezed and woken up, we gave Mr. C. a blank cheque pre-signed by my mother. He carefully filled in the amount. Back in the saddle, we emerged onto the road as from an underworld dream, not fully re-awakening until we were trotting smartly under the culvert. Jaunty now, we cantered along every slice of verge, sad to be away from the forge, sad to be away from Mr. C., glad to be away from that malevolent eyeball, glad to be away from the town.

'How was Mr. C.?' my mother would ask when we got home, country people once more. He was well, we'd say, and we'd tell her what he'd observed about the ponies' feet. She would nod. Mr. C. was almost God. What he observed, she remembered.

I don't know the date of Mr. C.'s death. I don't know where he's buried. When crucial people cease to be crucial, you talk about them, then cease to talk about them until, years later, you ask 'whatever happened to . . .' and wish you knew, though if Mr. C. died shrunken and fearful from dementia, I certainly don't want to know that.

The forge is still there, inevitably now a garage. Still dirty, still dishevelled, it's still a story-book cottage in search of a witch. Even amongst the engines and tyres, if I went in I might be totally immersed once more. A forge is so elemental that traces always cling. I don't go in. I don't need to. As with Mrs N.'s singing, the thump crunch of the hods and all the Not-So-Grand house's various complaints, I carry the forge with me.

22

GINGER BISCUITS

DOWN THE BACK drive, through the latched gate, across the field, over the stile into the railway field, over the railway, to the right of the track down towards the village was a black house. We never went near it – it didn't look welcoming – until the day the butcher's bay mare escaped onto the road and was hit by a car. It wasn't our car, but we were there, in our car, my mother driving, and we stopped, of course. My mother leaped out and went straight to the horse's head, gentling and soothing. We piled out after her. There was no blood. The mare simply stood, her off-side foreleg kinked at an unnatural angle, her eyes registering mild surprise. I don't remember the driver of the death-car. It wasn't their fault anyway, and I think once they'd seen my mother with the horse, they were, like the villagers who gathered, just spectators.

My mother issued orders. 'Find somebody with a telephone. Telephone the vet – his number will be in the book. Tell him to come at once. Find me a halter. And find Mr. A. I think the horse is his.' People must have scuttled off. We children were instructed to direct what traffic there was in those days. A halter materialised. People spoke in low tones. Would the horse like a blanket? No. Would she like a sugar-lump? Possibly. Will the vet put a splint on? Silence. Now the horse began to feel the pain, and static surprise gave way to fidgeting, her head swinging this way and that, then weariness outflanked fidgeting, then lassitude outflanked weariness and finally, when the full pain hit, her eyes dulled, her head sank, and though she was still physically upright, she sagged, resigned, it seemed, to her inevitable fate.

All this while my mother held the mare, her whole attention on the mare, stroking her nose and neck, only ceasing her murmuring to ask about success or not with contacting the vet, to answer questions she couldn't avoid and to try and quiet the noisy upset of the horse's owner, a rough, blustery man still wearing his butcher's apron. My mother held the mare until the vet arrived, and she held her when, after a brief inspection, he shook his head, produced his bolt-gun and shot the mare, my mother suddenly, shockingly, jumping back to avoid being crushed by the mare's instant collapse. Once the vet had gone and the corpse been tutted over, the crowd dispersed. We stayed, waiting for the blood-wagon which would take the corpse away, us and the blustery owner offering blustery commentary on the mare's possible escape tactics, the iniquities of the road and how his shop was being strangled by supermarkets.

A winch is used to haul a dead horse into a trailer. A winch was used in this case. After it was over, the wagon gone and the blustery man restored to butchery, a tall angular lady, grey hair escaping from a rough bun – later, when I saw pictures of Virginia Woolf, I thought they could have been sisters – brought over a mug and a tin. 'You'll be needin' tea,' she said to my mother in tones distinctly un-Virginia Woolf, 'and you'll all be needin' one a these.' The tea was sweet, the biscuits in the tin ginger. My mother accepted both. She wasn't shaking but she was shaken. Always wanting to put people at their ease she made conversation. The lady only smiled. When Ma had finished the tea, the old lady took the mug. 'Tek tin 'ome,' she said and climbed back up the path to the black house.

Those biscuits. They were punches of ginger, their sizes and thicknesses as uneven as the back-door flags so beloved of Mrs N. I didn't even like ginger, but I liked those biscuits. We decanted them and the next day Ma sent Second Sister and me down to return the tin. The door was open, so in we walked. That's how we became regular visitors to Union Pit House. Or half of it.

The house had been built as the headquarters of the Cliviger Coal Company and Miss M. lived with her brother, the Coal Company manager. His was a dying job, but after the last pit, Copy Pit, fully closed in 1963 and the gantries, winders and engine-houses were demolished, the old drifts and shafts still had to be managed, so Union Pit House remained, sticky black with the coaldust that for many in the village and beyond had constituted life itself. Miss M. wasn't employed by the pit. Her life had been spent walking to farms in all weathers to deliver babies and lay out the dead.

We quickly understood, or at least thought we understood, that brother and sister didn't get on. We never saw Mr. M., just occasionally heard movements. Eventually we learned that he was dead and had been dead for ages, though we weren't sure what 'ages' meant. A week? A month? A year? A decade? And if he was dead, who or what was moving about in the other half of the house? We couldn't ask because – an important detail I've omitted – Miss M. was stone deaf. We didn't want to alarm her, although she didn't seem like a person easily alarmed.

She didn't mention the horse that first time, or any time. Rightly or wrongly, we understood this was to signal that she and the village were separate. That suited us. We were separate from the village too. She was pleased we'd brought back her tin, less for the tin and more, I think, for the respect. She bid us sit, which we did, one on the floor, one in the chair opposite hers, all slowly roasting in front of the fire which burned winter and summer.

And so Miss M. began to 'belong' to us and we to her. We spoke through the medium of an exercise book in which we wrote down questions and told her what we'd been up to. She told us what we'd had for breakfast, something she gleaned from sniffing the air. 'Smelled sausages this morning,' she'd say, 'so I knew ye were back from yer school.' Always she'd tell us who in the village had died and if she forgot, we'd remind her.

'Anybody died, Miss M.?' She'd smile conspiratorially. 'There's allus somebody.'

She spoke slowly, her gaze sometimes on us then, as the years went by, more into the fire stoked high with the coal she was given as the dependent of a coalboard employee. Sometimes we'd remonstrate about the terrible burns that scabbed her legs when she fell asleep too close to the fire and she'd draw her legs back for a moment or two, then creep close again. There were silences. There was nodding. There was also snoozing. 'Yev bin asleep,' she'd say, and we'd smile sheepishly. 'Your house is so warm, Miss M., and ours is so cold!'

The biscuits appeared in industrial quantities from the kitchen, a lean-to affair across the yard, next to which was her bathroom shed – she had no indoor plumbing, a modern invention she deplored as unhygienic and unnecessary. There were biscuits to take home and biscuits to take to boarding school from where we wrote to her, but not enough.

One Christmas, maybe two, after Christmas lunch at home we ate Christmas dinner with Miss M., a testing, though joyous trial, not just for the quantities of food but because biscuits aside, Miss M. was no cook. Her sage and onion stuffing resembled something perished some time since. I tried not to think of her brother. To help us along we relied heavily on Brock, who afterwards took to visiting Miss M. on his own. He liked to eat dead things.

I want to tell you that Miss M. died in her own bed, with us, and the lady who eventually did her shopping, beside her. She didn't die like that. A couple of chancers arrived at Union Pit House. The woman explained, using her hands, that their car had boiled over so they'd left it, engine steaming, on the road. Could they have a jug of water? Miss M. walked over the yard to the kitchen to get what was needed. The man went with her while the woman nipped inside the house. A warming pan! Horse-brasses! Antique bits and bobs! They stole the lot, and with along with their loot they stole Miss M.'s tranquillity. She'd been asked for help. She'd given it. Her life had been built around that simple transaction. After the robbery she dwindled, then finally slipped and hurt herself so was taken into hospital where at least deafness spared her the sound of the nurses calling her by the first name even we didn't know – she was always Miss M. to us.

I have nightmares of unsympathetic nurses and slapdash care. Of lonely days and endless uncomforted nights. I could be wrong. Maybe kind nurses spent time with Miss M., made sure she was pain-free and creamed and bandaged her burned legs. I focus on the nurses to drown my own guilt. Once we'd left school, our visits were less frequent. When Miss M. died I was nineteen and in London. By the time the news reached me she was buried. I should have been there. I wasn't.

Union Pit House, sold, gentrified and re-named, is now hidden by leylandii. I suspect the sheds are long demolished. I'm sure the house now boasts a pristine kitchen and an ultra-hygienic bathroom. There'll be no smell of ginger. That's what happens, isn't it.

23

GOD'S CHOICE

L ETTING GO IS a strange old business. In the effort of putting things to bed as it were, some events you think long greyed out suddenly resurface in lively colour. It's unnerving, like being jolted awake when you've half dozed off. Still, nobody said letting go should be comfortable.

One summer holidays when I was about fourteen, I was standing at the kitchen window gazing at the logs in the log-shed. I didn't usually gaze at the logs. As you know, usually I was immersed in a book. This day, the day of the kitchen window, I had no book. I was treading water, adrift. At fourteen, the beginnings of impatience. Nothing so novelistic as 'waiting for life to begin', mine was a generalised impatience. I wasn't the person I wanted to be which was, at that moment, a person good at gym – being 'bendy' was the *sine qua non* of success at school – or at least able to do a front-drop on the trampoline, or catch a netball, or, closer to home, jump onto any horse and leap over any fence – be a rider like my mother in other words. Hormones, you may think. Alas not in my case. I was way behind on the hormone front. I didn't have a proper period until I was eighteen. So my impatience, as I remember it, was a kind of despondency. I was never going to be bendy. The trampoline front-drop would remain unconquered. I'd no chance of turning into Darrell in Malory Towers or Anne in *Fortune's Foal*. I was never even going to be recruited by freedom-fighters like Dick in *The Black*

Riders because freedom-fighters would never wander up the drive of the Not-So-Grand house which was, in any event, never going to be mine. As a girl, as a Towneley, as a human being, my destiny was to be ballast in the great ship of the world. Not splendid. Not awful. Just taking up space. Like the logs but not as useful.

I heard Brock before I saw him – he'd been loitering on the back stairs. His movement now was brisk and purposeful: down the stairs, a right turn into the scullery and directly out of the back door. My gaze sharpened. On top of the log-shed was a hutch, home to Second Sister's guinea-pigs, only the hutch wasn't there. Second Sister had taken it into the garden to give Castor and Pollux a run. She'd been anxious about our resident murderer and shut him away. He'd escaped, and whilst as yet unaware of the unhutched guinea-pigs, he was heading to the path round the house that would eventually lead straight to them. My internal route to the guinea-pigs was shorter than Brock's external. I only had to run through the kitchen, through the door to the front of the house, up Great Granny's stairs, past the library, left through the hall and out of the garden doors where 'Brock!' I would cry and Second Sister would immediately hussle the guinea-pigs to safety. I saw myself running. I heard myself shouting. I imagined the safety. Yet I neither ran nor shouted because I was suddenly gripped, paralysed even, by the realisation that at this moment I was not ballast. Far from it. Brock and the guinea-pigs had gifted me the greatest power in the world, the power of life and death. It was like being God. Indeed at this moment I was God. I held the fate of those guinea-pigs in the palm of my hand.

Then something unexpected. Contrary to everything the nuns taught us, being all-powerful God didn't make me warm and loving. Being God made me unaccountable, unreasonable, arbitrary, capricious. I could run and save. I could stay and condemn. A simple choice and mine to make.

At the guinea-pigs' funeral I intoned the chosen prayers along with the others. I scattered flowers on the graves. I helped Second Sister haul the hutch back onto the log-shed roof. Rinsing earth from our hands at the kitchen sink, Second Sister crying, I couldn't stop staring at the logs. How precisely they were stacked, each log wedged carefully against its neighbour. The stacker of those logs had also made choices. He could have simply tossed the logs in an ugly jumble. He could have left them outside to rot. Instead he had chosen to make something beautiful. I felt ashamed. I wanted to turn the clock back and make a different choice. But not actually being God, the guinea pigs remained dead and I remained ballast, only ballast who had done something irredeemably mean.

24

ELEMENTAL GAMBLES

DAMP, SHIVERY, HANDS clammy, feet icy, the prospect of landing ignominiously in bog very close and the prospect of home pretty distant: if you've never been out hunting it may sound the worst thing in the world. I loved it. And I don't mean post 2004 'hunting', castrated hunting, designer hunting, hunting-by-numbers. I mean the real hunting of Sassoon and Trollope, of Somerville and Ross, of Surtees. I mean hunting that brought you face to face with yourself because however many books about it you read, however many dreams you had, once you'd climbed into the saddle, settled your stirrups, gathered the reins and grappled with the thong and lash of your whip, just as the weather was just the weather, so you were just you, the horse was just the horse, and facing you both a bundle of questions, all unanswerable.

Would there be good scent? Would hounds find and run? Would the day bring glory - exemplary manners (me and horse); horse jumping cleverly; me staying aboard; twilight hacking back to the bone-shaker landrover close enough behind the huntsman to overhear his chirrupy, grumbly, homeward conversation with his hounds? Or would the day bring shame - horse bolting or barging; horse not jumping, me falling off; losing hounds; plodding back to base alone or with some other bungler? Nobody, from the huntsman right down to me, knew the answers for themselves or anybody else. After hounds were called together and we trotted off, it was just 'this riding and tumbling . . . this being blown upon and rained upon and splashed from head to foot with mud'[*] and over all this blowing and raining and splashing hovered the prospect of death, animal and human, sometimes very close up, sometimes a little further way, but always hovering.

Death was the elemental gamble which elevated hunting from an enjoyable gallop across country to something serious and primal. Death generated the emotional tangle that was part and parcel of hunting, the irreconcilable conundrum of running with the hare – please God, escape! – and hunting with the hounds – please God, don't let hounds be disappointed! Death was the reason, so my mother taught us, that, like marriage, hunting was 'not to be under-taken unadvisedly or lightly; but reverently, discreetly, advisedly, soberly, and in the fear of God'. Or at least in fear of the huntsman and fieldmaster. Death meant that hunting wasn't a fudge, an 'all must have prizes' affair. Out hunting there were winners and losers and nothing in between.

My mother loved hunting for itself and also because out hunting she returned to the self she'd curbed when she married: an instinc-tive self, alert, aware, given to darting after beauty – in full school uniform, we once wildly trespassed after an implausible hoopoe – a self directed by what touched her heart and spoke to her imagi-nation. Out hunting, she was considered brave because uncertain ground, bottomless bogs, wire, treacherous hedges or unforgiving walls with hidden ditches on the landing side didn't frighten her. Really, it was less fearlessness and more the relish of autonomy. Out hunting she made her own decisions, her only concerns the hounds and her horse, and she had more faith in the latter than she had in any human, including my father and the pope. Only the vet and the farrier were near contenders.

Along with other sisters, I hunted from an early age and though

* *Vogue*, March 1926, Virginia Woolf 'The Life of John Mytton'

we took our mother's lessons to heart, at first it was all about staying on and keeping up. Later, when staying on and keeping up wasn't such a challenge, we looked outwards. We learned about the relationship between hunter and hunted; how what you see of nature masks what's hidden. We learned how hounds work. Important, all that, and I suppose this is why, driving to the meet with my mother, we didn't confide, mother to daughter, daughter to mother. We spoke of the day ahead, discussed whether to get a lorry (we did in the end – the warmth! the comfort!); decided where best to park; gazed anxiously at the weather; deliberated whether this horse or that should wear this or that; and wondered why tail bandages always vanish. Nothing memorable.

Some part of me now wishes that as I got older I'd pushed that nothing into something, that I'd used those many bone-shaking hours to ask about my mother's childhood; about my grandparents, whose marriage I rather idealised; and, of course, that Great Unanswerable, about why she'd married my father. I doubt she'd have welcomed deeper conversations. Hunting was away from all that stuff.

It wasn't as if the time was unproductive. We used quite a bit of it to make inroads into the Turkish cigarettes, oval and untipped, that my father, a non-smoker except of cigars, had sent up from London each month because the boxes were handsome and he liked the smell.

Smoking was not a new chore. Sometimes remaining in their own handsome box, sometimes decanted into silver boxes, the cigarettes decorated the drawing room and as soon as we graduated from the nursery my father encouraged us to help ourselves. The first couple of smokes were like leaping onto a thoroughbred before you'd mastered an old pony: you felt proudly sophisticated and unproudly sick. If a cigarette occasionally took my mother's fancy or she wanted to lend a smoking hand, she elegantly extricated strands of tobacco from her teeth with her thumb and first finger. We children just spat. When the task seemed beyond us, we asked friends to help. Often they'd been bribed not to smoke until they were twenty-one and our reasoning that untipped Turkish cigarettes were more exotic fruits than tobacco was never very convincing. Usually we puffed away on our own. We didn't want to disappoint our father and smoking did look rather cool, even with the spitting. On hunting mornings my mother and I would sometimes manage four between us. It wasn't much, but it showed willing.

On the homeward journey we ditched the cigarettes and ate scrambled egg and bacon rolls, sometimes in the rich silence of a day to be savoured, sometimes in the gloomy silence of a day best forgotten. In either case, arriving back in the yard and exchanging the warm fug of the cab for the dark chill of the yard was a foretaste of purgatory. Circulation limping, eyes heavy and mouth dry if we'd forgotten the tea Thermos, one of us had to stagger across the meadow to the house to fetch the pans of linseed and barley to add to the horses' mashes. The meadow was big and hilly. The pans were heavy and full. You were tired. If you'd taken a fall you were a bit battered. But even through the post-hunting myriad of horse-chores, even whilst carting all those pans from the house and all the tack back to be cleaned – the weight of it! – I never wanted a groom. For all its human discomforts and inconveniences – unhelpful lighting, no hot water, one lethargic cold water tap (frozen most of the winter), no telephone, no tack room, for years no loo – in fact as desperate a stable yard as you can imagine – still, the cracking paint, ill-fitting doors, lop-sided bolts, missing windows and dripping gutters were ours, the imperfections reassuringly mirroring our own.

Near to midnight on a hunting day I'd return to the yard. With the two stable yard cottages tightly curtained so little threat of interruption, I could slip unseen around the post-hunting relaxings of the horses, their heads drooping, lower lips softly sagging, one back leg resting. Bonded by the whole shared history of the day, I was the spirit-in-the-yard, straightening rugs, settling beds, checking water buckets, murmuring nonsense because it was just me and them, them and me, and it was what I liked to do.

And over the yard, over the horses, over me, over the day and all future days, presided the midden, smoking like the chimney in Peter Pan. I was at one with that midden. I never felt more content than when making it, tending it, squaring it off. Hunting was hunting, and I still miss it. Even more, sometimes with almost inexplicable longing, I miss the satisfaction of standing on top of that midden. Tired, limbs aching, hands and face stinging with cold, it's a foretaste of heaven to contemplate the moon as your feet warm nicely in an orderly pile of ever-welcoming, gently steaming, slowly decomposing muck.

25

OLD FRIENDS

FIRST MENTION OF the Not-So-Grand house is of a keeper's cottage. In 1559, when hearing Mass became illegal, local Catholics gathered there for 'clandestine worship', the priest using a folding altar whose day job was acting as a wardrobe. Few fragments of that cottage survive but you'd be forgiven for thinking that at least some contents of its kitchen had not only survived, they'd found their way into our fridge.

After we no longer had a cook, my mother unwillingly took over the kitchen. It may have been partly in protest that she kept food past old, past vintage, past even basic recognition. One useful, if unintended, consequence: we children developed lifelong immunity to food poisoning. The year the whole of our boarding school was poleaxed by refrozen chicken, my sisters and I suffered not even a rumble.

If my mother's relationship with the kitchen was hostile, her relationship with food was wildly contradictory. She hated waste, yet had a visceral need to shop in monstrous quantities in the futile, never entirely extinguished hope of never having to go shopping again. The monstrous quantities turned both fridge and larder into mortuaries, the fresh piled onto the not-so-fresh, cooked meat onto uncooked meat. Hanging from hooks there were always gamebirds passed plucking. Splodged into tubs was fruit passed even bottling or jam. She kept egg boxes of recent eggs perched atop three or four dusty and oxidised tins of eggs presumably left over from the war. Out of curiosity, after our mother died we scrambled the tinned eggs. I don't think they were delicious. Still, it would take more than rusty eggs to kill children brought up on sheep's brains and used to eating cheese not considered 'over' until it had walked itself off the table.

The danger of this mortuary approach is obvious: soup. Anything is fair game for soup, so soup was where much of the mortuary ended up, as did all bones, some picked clean, some not quite so clean, collected from all the plates at the end of every bony meal. Visitors unused to the mortuary approach soon got the hang of it. At the siren call of 'stock!' all plates were whisked into the kitchen and all remains scraped into the double-handled steel pot, the new remains squelched on top of the old. Once my mother was satisfied that nothing plate-wise had escaped, she added salt and bay leaves plus, from the larder's huge vats, the mush that had once been leeks or courgettes. Soup candidates from the fridge were granted a perfunctory sniff and momentary consideration of 'sweet or savoury, do you think?' No answer was expected. In the Not-So-Grand house stockpot there was no separation of sheep from goats.

A survivor from my great-grandmother's day – not that she ever saw the kitchen – the stockpot itself was antediluvian and venerable. Also not-so-grand. Warped decades before, the lid balanced on top of the stockpot's already kinked lip like an old LP you can't bear to throw out. The lid's handle had broken and what remained shuggled and shook. Lifting it was a risky business. The pot's handles were equally reduced, their heat-resistant silicone chipped away leaving small loose stubs which, given the weight of the pot both empty and full, were also a gamble. Unless, like removal-men with a heavy armchair, you lifted the pot from the bottom, you were likely to end up with stock inside your shoes.

Once everything possible had been crammed in, my mother topped up with water and stuck the pot on the Aga to boil. 'I'm just waiting for the stock,' she'd say, and sometimes she did. Other times the telephone rang, or she got bored, or went off to do something else 'just for a minute' and then the stockpot would be forgotten and left to blow its lid clean off. If my mother did manage to wait, then at the first sign of bubbles she'd shove the pot into the top lefthand oven for at least twenty-four hours. Or that was the idea. But the stockpot in the oven was even less likely to be remembered than the stockpot on the hotplate, so by the time it was retrieved, days, possibly weeks, later, its contents were more brown sludge than stock. Still, when the sludge was manhandled into the voluminous stock sieve, whatever managed to trickle through was added to the ongoing stock that sat in a green (or had once been green) plastic bowl in the fridge. Uncovered, the stock fat rose to the top to be skimmed off at intervals with the fish slice.

I learned later that you're supposed to make soup with stock, i.e. that the stock itself is not supposed to be soup. At the Not-So-Grand house that distinction wasn't made. The stock was soup, the soup was stock. We drank it every night because my father loved soup. It also pleased him to cock a snook at the hypocrisy of his step-father who, on his return from the Bank of England, had had personal soup sent up to his room so as to avoid comparison with a plutocratic banker troughing his three or four course dinner. 'If he had soup in his room, nobody else could have any,' my father said, the memory still bitter. Everybody should have soup. Let them eat soup.

It was a piece of luck for my mother that she died before my father discovered lovage. Lovage throws out yellow blooms in June. My father ignored these. He was after the green leaves, collecting mounds in a basket and bearing them to the kitchen with the satisfaction of a successful truffle-hunter. It's hard to describe the consistency of his lovage soup. Mottled green, faintly gritty, stickily gelatinous – warm slurry comes to mind. The grittiness was surprising since lovage's leaves and stems are glabrous, a Jabberwockian word that means hairless. Whatever the glabrous grittiness, the lovage was so abundant that not only did my father fill the fridge with his slurry, he pressed us to take buckets of the stuff away.

In Ukraine, so I read, lovage is considered an aphrodisiac. In the Not-So-Grand house, everyone except my father considered it poison. Why I couldn't tell my father that I'd rather face real slurry than lovage slurry I don't know. Perhaps I hoped the slurry might improve. It never did.

Over our childhoods, supermarkets crept into Burnley, almost overnight displacing the independent shops. At first blush we were glad. Supermarkets meant we no longer had to stand, mortified, in the greengrocer's, trying to ignore the mutterings of customers who wanted one apple or a couple of bananas as my mother took her time – 'I think I'll have fifteen of those, Mr. H.'. My mother did sympathise with the frustrations of those in the queue behind her, but not only did she clear the shelves, she couldn't leave without asking after the raspberry crop here and the prospect for gooseberries there. It could drive you mad.

Not as mad as the most cursed invention of all time, the supermarket sell-by date. Most people used the sell-by date as a guide to edibility. My mother used it as a bargain basement. With no discernible discrimination she bought whatever could no longer be offered in the store: lumps of luminous processed cheese; fizzy rhubarb yoghurt; watery bacon; dessicated cakes; strange-smelling offal; vegetables already half way to soup. She still drew the line at sliced bread but plastic sausages were piled into the boot of the car, and the boot was big.

My father bypassed sell-by dates in the same way as he bypassed any hint of a 'ready meal', whether in-date or out: he simply ate cream. Cream was the alpha; cream was the omega. Cream was the question; cream the answer. As a nod to something – certainly not health, about which he never concerned himself until he passed 100 – he'd occasionally include a hint of scallop or a cornflake or two. Mainly, though, he just ate cream. Sometimes, when we were still sitting round the dinner table putting off the dreaded chore of clearing up, my father would rise, return with wine and cream and consume equal quantities of both. My mother would watch. She didn't want cream. She wanted marmalade. Layering relics from larder or fridge – spinach, rice-pudding, paté, junket, pickle, apple crumble – she created marmalade-topped gothic novels in a bowl. 'Would you like some?' she'd ask. We never said yes. Old friends are all very well. Eating old friends is all very well. Covering them in marmalade isn't all very well.

'Do you remember the food of your childhood?' somebody asked me the other day.

'I do,' I said, 'it became unforgettable.'

'Childhood food is always the best,' the somebody said.

I wasn't sure how to reply. 'Childhood food is certainly something,' I said in the end. 'I'm sometimes surprised to find I'm still alive.'

26

THE ENEMY WITHIN

TEENAGERS ARE TRADITIONALLY at war with their parents. It was quite hopeless going to war with my mother. She had no quarrel with us. My father was more bellicose and rated his enemies in order of exasperation. In this list, teenage children came fourth.

By this time, enemy number one was firmly fixed: the horses. To my father, the horses weren't just Enemy One, they were the Eternal Enemy. They were also enemies with complications. Whereas to him the horses were intrusions, interruptions, intolerable and permanent irritants, to my mother they were truth, beauty, joy and delight. How do you fight truth, beauty, joy and delight? My father never discovered. Nonetheless, he never gave up.

His main complaint was that the horses always came first. My mother's defence was robust. It wasn't her fault that the stables, being across the large meadow, were too far from the house to hear my father shout or the telephone ring. It wasn't her fault that it was impossible to nip across the meadow to perform even the smallest horse chore – are there really any small horse chores? – without the breakfast bacon burning to ashes.

You might have thought an accommodation would be reached. My father might make his own breakfast. My mother might choose a cooler oven for the bacon. But my mother didn't care enough about the bacon and my father's strategy was resolutely to do nothing, and do it furiously, a strategy doomed yet never abandoned. Horses were the slipperiest element of his slippery slope. His grandmother had left no guidance. It was just his luck that it was through horses that my mother fell in love with unlovely-to-many north-east Lancashire: real, solid, granite-based love for the place to which marriage had brought her and to which the Towneley name bound her.

If horses were Enemy One, weeds came a close second. For my father, weeding was never a boring chore needing only the casual weaponry of a gardener's kneeling mat, Christmas-present gloves and a pair of secateurs. Weeding was bare-knuckle combat of ferocious darts and snatches. Attacks could be launched at any time of the day or night, in whatever clothes he was wearing – uniforms from honorary this or honourable that, Savile Row suits and, unless in his pyjamas, always a tie.

His preferred method was the full-throttle seize/drag/yank, his square fingers strengthened to vices by decades of playing the 'cello. When the weeds fought back, his yanking was fuelled by an enmity verging on insanity. Aged 100 he would still pit his whole standing weight against an unwanted stem or sucker, then drop to his knees for better purchase, yapping imprecations like Brock insulting the priest. As we grew taller and stronger we would be summoned as yanking reinforcement – 'get hold of THAT will you' – and if 'THAT' was thorny or poisonous, there was no waiting for you to fetch gloves. This was war! Nobody waited for GLOVES. Victims were dragged onto the lawn and, like Hector outside the walls of Troy, left exposed until the gardening equivalent of King Priam came to gather them up for burial or burning. My father never did Gardener Priam's job himself. If we were between Priams, the weeds remained decomposing in plain sight. Dead, this enemy was invisible.

Not so Enemy Three, the rabbits, but they were seldom dead. Our childhood fear of the rifle muzzle poking out of the dressing room window was very real, though as we grew older, along with the dogs and even the rabbits, we took only marginal care. Had my father hit something, along with howls there would have been astonished applause.

We children were enemy number four. Enemy is too strong a word. Young children were a nuisance. As we grew up we were less a nuisance and more adversaries against whom to refresh the combative skills of the Oxford tutorial. Had my father played tennis, even against a novice child he'd never have conceded a point.

Any mention of reading activated a particularly hair-trigger adversarial laser-switch. 'I've just been reading XXX,' I might try, hoping to impress. It's some kind of curse that however old you are, the wish to impress your father never quite vanishes.

'Oh? And have you read YYY?' [obscure book, or expensive hardback recently reviewed in the *TLS* or *LRB*]. He could pretty much guarantee I hadn't.

'Not yet.'

'Really.'

When accompanied by a gentle upward inflection and a forward tilt of the head, 'really' can be warmly encouraging. My father's 'really' was neither warm nor encouraging. My father's 'really', always pronounced 'rarely', was an Exocet zinger against which you needed a shield as yet unforged by man. It was a blessing that, like the weeds, once you were conquered, he didn't give you another thought.

Or so I supposed. Imagine my surprise when one afternoon he turned round and asked 'Have I been a good father?'

He'd halted outside the library. I halted too. We stood together in front of the big chest with drawers nobody opened and on top of which the drinks bottles gathered dust, all except the whisky. Had I not been so taken aback by a question I simply couldn't imagine my father ever asking, I might have asked why he wanted to know. Or, had my mother not been laid out upstairs ready for the undertaker, I might have laughed. But I was taken aback, my mother was laid out upstairs and I was far from laughing.

Until that moment I had imagined my father's thoughts, like mine, were entirely focused on what was about to happen. In less than fifteen minutes my mother would be leaving the Not-So-Grand house for the last time. Resplendent in the long coat-dress of cream and gold she'd worn at Sixth Sister's wedding, her cancer-pain finally gone, our loss-pain was just beginning.

My father lightly dusted the bottles with his handkerchief. In his grief, the dusting seemed to afford him an odd kind of comfort. Still, grief or not, dusting or not, he was waiting for answer.

What is a 'good' father? It's too enormous a question, and too subjective, to answer in general or even at all. For a start, we all have different concepts of 'good'. Certainly, my father wasn't a comfortable father. To be a comfortable father you have to be a comfortable person. My father's childhood of rejections and discardings had solidified discomfort. For some men, decades of steady and steadfast marriage might have allowed comfort to seep through. My father wasn't such a man.

But there were cracks. Of course there were. When thinking of my father now, I like to remember him away from horses, weeds and rabbits, away, even, from the Not-So-Grand house and his task of being a Towneley. My best memories are of him abroad, particularly when, after my mother's death, he took a daughter with him, sometimes one of the others, sometimes me.

In Paris, Rome or Venice, or even closer to home in London, he forgot he was my father and thus also an adversary. Instead, at restaurants it was his delight to discover – nobody had a better restaurant nose – we could lunch or dine like strangers arbitrarily thrown together by chance or happy circumstance. Always one to order another bottle, hours could pass not entirely unbarbed, but with Exocet zingers fewer and fired more gently as we chatted about problems and puzzles both contemporary and perennial, like the nature of political authority or the value of gossip. If carefully steered, he might also speak of his early introduction to music or his time as a prisoner-of-war.

There was, though, one big gap: any interest in our lives away from the Not-So-Grand house, or, in time, the lives of his grandchildren and great-grandchildren. He never asked about, and I never dreamed of bringing up, any personal problem, be it emotional, financial or practical. I never sought his advice, solicited help, not even for a lift to the railway station. To advise and help anybody, most of all the people most intimately connected to you, you first have to get to know them. You get to know them best by listening. My father didn't know how to listen.

And so, standing outside the library, my father dusting, my mother dead and the three of us waiting for the undertaker, I was a bit stuck.

My father shook out his handkerchief. 'Well?'

'You're a father,' I offered.

'Really,' he said.

We left it at that.

27

ANTLER RATTLING

ALONG WITH THE string quartets and other musicians, visitors of all kinds poured into the Not-So-Grand house, sometimes not pouring out in the same numbers. A friend of Only Brother's stayed for weeks beyond Only Brother's return to boarding school. Had my father noticed he might well have taken Extraneous Boy to be Only Brother. As it was, nobody noticed, or noticed enough to make any remark. Perhaps Extraneous Boy is still there. Our friends came, some only once. Being a guest in the Not-So-Grand house could be an uneasy undertaking.

Eccentric relations weren't a problem. We could cope with any number of them. Within weeks of discovering that a cousin was growing yoghurt in wine glasses on the window of the bedroom always known as 'Lady Norman's room', my mother was growing yoghurt herself, not in wine-glasses - too small when you've seven children - in large pots in the airing cupboard. For a while she was yoghurt-obsessed. Searching in store-cupboards for loo-paper or anchovies it was hard to avoid pots, bowls, jugs of the stuff, some of it so long forgotten it was only recognisable because what else could it once have been?

Childhood friends were different and our teenage friends different again. My mother welcomed them all, at least in theory. In practice she couldn't tell them apart. My father didn't like the idea of our friends, whether old or young. But ever the combatant, our teenage friends at least afforded opportunity for a joust.

His favourite jousting-ground was the schoolroom, his favourite time, dinner. Before a friend had started on their soup, a brave effort if they knew anything of the soup's provenance, my father would ask in the guileless tones usually associated with enquiries about holiday plans, something like 'do you think William Pitt and Margaret Thatcher have anything in common?'. The questionee, transfixed by the charming smile, would reach quickly for either the only fact they knew about Pitt or what they thought was a clever return: 'Do you mean the older Pitt or the younger, sir?'

My father was ready, his smile not quite so smiley. 'If I'd meant Chatham, I'd have said so.'

At that moment the joust could go two ways. The questionee could mutter an admission that their ignorance about Pitt was unforgiveable and relapse into awkward silence, or they could embark on a stream of verbiage that revealed they knew something about both Pitt and Thatcher though nothing either original or interesting. In the former case, my father's face registered utter boredom; in the latter he would let his victim run on for quite a bit before that magisterially dismissive 'Really?' cut them off at the knees. If there's a victorious way to finish soup, my father finished his soup victoriously.

You might think that our invitations to schoolfriends, and later to boyfriends, or those we hoped might become boyfriends, would have included a warning or, failing a warning, we might catapult to the rescue. We did neither. The excitement of a joust is to see who falls first. With surprise on his side, my father had the advantage but there was always a sporting chance, just the tiniest, that the friend might triumph. When triumph came, it came trailing clouds of glory.

Visitor triumphs were fewer than they might have been because most laboured under a basic misapprehension: that to impress my father and win over my mother they had to know things, actual things, facts and so-on. In truth, as we grew up it became clear that no conversation was ever going to be based on what you knew, and facts, well, who cared about them. Round the Not-So-Grand house table the most important thing, indeed the only thing, was still, as it had always been, and with no quarter given to guests, not to be dull. However many facts you supplied, however many books you'd read, however esoteric your knowledge, if you were deemed dull, that was the end of you. This didn't mean we children weren't dull: it just meant we had a pathological fear of it. Fear adds quite an edge to jousting.

When she could be persuaded to stop fossicking in the kitchen and sit down with or without her marmaladed bowl of relics, our mother was a keen jouster, her sparring laced with those secret welts and scratches invisible to any outsider, including children closer to their parents than we were to ours, that scar every marriage. Over dinner – always religiously at 8 p.m. – she would take a position and hang onto it more to deny my father the satisfaction of winning than from any unshakeable belief. With no hope of capitulation by anybody, hours passed and it was often long after midnight before an uneasy truce was declared. When visitors arrived, at the very least they were fresh troops.

The perceptive guest realised early that whilst survival depended on a defensive strategy, to flourish you needed your own plan of attack. An obvious opening gambit was to bat a casual question at my father before he had time to gather his own weapons. The danger lay in choosing a subject about which it was reasonably safe to assume that my father knew nothing, only to find yourself neatly unhorsed by his 'why on earth would I know anything about that?' Best, if trickier, to choose a topic about which my father would feel he ought to know something, so wouldn't want to admit ignorance. Even then, victory would be touch and go. If my father felt in danger of losing, he would summon the heavy artillery. 'Don't you agree?' he'd demand of everybody except his adversary. It was a stamp, not a question.

Occasionally my father would open a new front. I'm thinking

of an evening in the early 1980s. Eldest Sister, Second Sister and I, plus various friends, were mustered in the drawing room. My father sat quite still, pretending to read. At around quarter past seven, safe in the knowledge that my mother was in the kitchen so couldn't countermand, he announced, as though in passing and to no-one in particular, 'I think we might change for dinner tonight'.

Just as he'd hoped, mass consternation. Some of the men had dinner-jackets but hadn't brought them – why would they? This was the 1980s! Others had either never had one or, feeling themselves radical, had discarded them as stuffy.

My father was gracious to those who had a dinner-jacket but hadn't brought it, musing, with spiky whimsy, about what kind of people assumed, even in a Not-So-Grand house, that they wouldn't change for dinner? To those who'd never had one, he made no remark. The radicals fared worst. My father would listen to their reasoning as though indulging primary school children before, with the deflating kindness that kills, he'd say 'Well there we are. I won't change either'. In their dreams, most of the radicals probably declared 'change, don't change, your world is ending, old man'. In real life they looked at their feet. All except one. Let's call him James.

James arrived late at the Not-So-Grand house. Irritated by his lateness and scenting blood, my father didn't hesitate to fire his 'change for dinner' gun. Instead of looking at his feet, James looked my father straight in the eye. 'Good idea, sir,' he said. 'I haven't brought a dinner-jacket but you look like a man with two. Perhaps I could borrow one?' This marked the end of the dinner-jacket strategy. The new strategy was music.

With hawk-eyed patience my father waited for somebody to wander up to the piano. At once, the weaponised charm – 'Do you play?' People who wander up to pianos do tend to play, and as soon as there was any kind of nod, my father would present them with a score. Minutes later the pianist would find themselves settled on the piano stool, my father with his 'cello a few feet away. 'Let's begin.'

The sightreading challenge was testing. Many couldn't bring

themselves to start. Others started and faltered – 'sorry, so sorry'. My father feigned understanding tolerance. When things ground to a halt, with pained exasperation he shook his head. How silly to play the piano if you couldn't sightread! What was the piano for except chamber-music? Playing the piano alone was a ridiculous thing to do. This preposterous assertion left the pianist too dumbstruck to say so much as 'hang on'. Sighing, my father removed himself and his 'cello from the room and for the rest of the pianist's visit music was never referred to again. After the pianist's departure, my father pronounced his verdict: 'completely unmusical, and seemed to know nothing about the piano. Don't you agree?' Alas for my father, as with dinner-jackets, this strategy too came to an abrupt end. There's always one. Let's call him Douglas.

Douglas was a friend of mine. Shrewd, sharp and funny, he'd just come out publicly as gay so was in cheerful mood. No bother there. My father picked his prejudices, and gayness wasn't one of them. Whatever the pope decreed, what people did by mutual consent in their own time was entirely up to them. It was only when Douglas wandered up to the piano that my father's eyes sparked. He presented the music. 'Shall we?'

'Do let's!' Douglas played the introduction. The marking was allegro. He followed it. He let my father struggle along for a bit before stopping. Now Dougie's eyes sparked. 'Would you like me to take it a little slower?' That marked the end of the music strategy. Best stick to the Exocet 'really' zinger. Nobody could beat that.

Straightforward and requiring no preliminaries, zingers were sometimes aimed at grandchildren. It was sad that my father either couldn't see, or refused to see, that whilst his own children had grown used to them, grandchildren found zingers disconcerting, sometimes upsetting. Or perhaps he could see that very well but considered being an amiable grandfather a dangerous lurch down the slippery slope. As it was, the grandchildren's visits to the Not-So-Grand house reminded me of my visits to my 'dead' grandfather: conversation but no real connection. Still, if against his grandchildren

my father took his antler-rattling too far, it gives me some pleasure
to recall that on at least two occasions during peak antler-rattling
time, antlers were rattled back.

28

WHITEWAYS, BLACKWAYS, MIREY WAYS

WHEN MY MOTHER'S 'real' life really began, that is to say when 'eventually eventually eventually' truly became 'now now now' – in other words when she'd had the babies, endured the house, mastered school uniforms, worn hats when required, counted the laundry out and counted it all back – the life that became her life's work began without fanfare. She was president of the local NSPCC. The charity needed money. 'I'll organise a sponsored ride,' she said. She knew the bureaucracy would be tedious. As for settling the route, how hard could that be? She now rode every day, the moors open to all. It turned out that the moors were not open to all. They were open to us because of our name and because of the estate. For others, routes were stymied by locked gates, mired bridleways, barbed wire and machinery strategically abandoned to stop 'trespassers'. Even many of the old green lanes were impassable, their footprints degraded or vanished or simply forgotten. My mother was puzzled. Over the blockages, she was angry. Why were there blockages? Who had encouraged/allowed such a thing? Surely for centuries most of these routes had been packhorse trails, their use uncontested? Then the question all sensible people dread: what could be done?

Thus began the era of maps. We sat on maps; we ate on maps. There were maps in the flower room; maps in the schoolroom; maps in the kitchen; my mother's sitting room was carpeted with maps. Open a cupboard and maps tumbled out. Maps were plastered on every surface not taken up by something else, and often the something else was covered with maps. Maps were glued above the telephone. Maps hid the dogs' beds. Maps were squashed into pockets. Maps were laminated, folded, rammed into waterproof wallets and attached to saddles. We no longer simply rode, we were no longer even riders; we were now explorers sallying forth into the 'known unknown' world of packhorse trails, of drovers' tracks, of limers' gates and corpse roads. These explorations increased in duration and intensity after my mother survived her first bout of cancer when, despite all the horrors of treatment, she launched into long distance racing. She was still alive and going to make the most of it.

Now the explorations had a dual purpose: rediscovery and retracing on the one hand; training herself and her horse for competitions on the other. My mother did nothing with half a heart. Overnight, 'explorations' morphed into the full-throttle quest.

Questing always began with a soon-to-be-familiar untruth. 'We'll be a couple of hours,' my mother would state cheerfully. 'I just want to look at ....' quick squint at map, quick comparison with another map, quick consultation with photograph followed by a not-at-all quick telephone call to another packhorse route obsessive (like bees swarming, obsessives find each other). She'd finish the sentence with triumph: 'I just want to look at the old way that must run between A and B.' We soon learned to read 'must' as 'may' or 'possibly' or 'could have, once upon a time'.

Ma was undaunted and undauntable. 'It's the obvious route for the jaggermen. Look – through the broadgate, up this rake – see where it follows the line of the hill – and a stoop's been marked here, and' – this with the thrill of Howard Carter in pursuit of Egyptian tombs – 'I'm told three setts have been found along the bit of blackway that's left and where there's three there must be more'.

The excitement was palpable. It wasn't just the natural excitement of feeling her way, squelchy step by squelchy step over a seemingly trackless waste, or of uncovering evidence of old routes, stone by stone. The real excitement was in conjuring, through language, stories and physical immersion, the hidden world of causeways and holloways, of cloughs and royds, of clapper bridges and clam bridges, of spandrels and stangs, of hushings and jumbs, of grips and whams. My mother's excitement was infectious. Riding with her, you couldn't help but feel one of the gang of Galloway ponies, packs secured by broad webbing belts known as wantas, not so much following the map as following the bells of the steady 'gal' (short for Galloway, not girl) who'd earned, after many miles and journeys, his or her place as leader.

Pursuing the ghosts of packhorses past was no daydreamy dawdle. Questing meant riding beyond far horizons in weather so seldom kind that retracing the quests on foot after our mother's death we couldn't understand why everything seemed so unfamiliar until we realised that the sun was shining. Also, we were unencumbered by my mother's questing luggage: those proliferating maps, plus paper, pen, hoofpick, baler-twine for rickety gates, wire-cutters 'just in case'. Then there was the camera. Lord how we hated our mother's camera. 'I'll just take a picture here' is the worst sentence in the world when rain is trickling down your neck and your boots leak. At least in those days she couldn't instantly message one of her fellow obsessives. If she'd lived into the era of mobile phones, I might have strangled her.

We still sometimes rode where we pleased. More often, though, our riding now had purpose. As seafarers navigate sequences of stars, so we were ground-readers, our horses hopping and skipping like gazelles, ears sometimes pricked, sometimes more quizzically arranged as we tried to determine, through going soft and hard, tracked and untracked, rough (mostly) and smooth (seldom) where the prints of long-dead ponies and mules might have fallen. Grooved and rutted from decades of iron-shod hooves and iron-bound cartwheels,

occasional causey-stones offered clues. This way! No, unlikely as it
seems, that way! Charting these often-perfidious relics of history
it was impossible not fancifully to hear, along with the gals' bells,
all the massed hustle and jingly bustle of packman and pack-beast
striving to keep their feet and their tempers amid the general churn
of unmade roads. Once the backbone of Britain, their arrivals and
departures as significant as births and deaths, we remember few
of the packmen's names. But here were their marks, there their
indentations, and everywhere the views they probably didn't see
as, heads down, shoulders hunched, they wound their way round,
through and over desolate terrain that tolerated but never welcomed.

If we weren't around – school, then eventually work – my mother
would quest on her own. It was on those lonely questings that I
think she felt most fulfilled. Marriage, children, official duties with
my father – he was first High Sheriff, then Lord Lieutenant – had
swept her up and along, always at somebody else's behest. Hunting
was one escape, but seasonal. Out on an unfamiliar moor with her
compass and her maps, she was free in all seasons to sweep herself
as her researches and fancy took her. It wasn't that the physical
hardship, the unwarrantable weather, the likelihood of getting utterly
lost, the risk, on unstable ground, of getting bogged or stuck was
some kind of challenging 'me time'. The very idea of 'me time' would
have appalled her. Her fulfilment lay in being where others and their
horses had been, she and her horse adding, however imperceptibly,
to the script of valiant human endeavour. That was fulfilment, and
it was deep and unshakeable.

Her mark was not so imperceptible. Unlike the packmen whose
names are lost, as I mentioned at the start of this memoir, my
mother's name is enshrined in the Mary Towneley loop, the forty-
eight mile circular loop at the South Pennine end of the Pennine
Bridleway National Trail. The whole trail runs for 205 miles. My
mother investigated and documented every inch.

In the preface of Titus Thornber's *Seen on the Packhorse Trails*
my mother wrote 'Readers . . . will want to ride or walk in the

footsteps of Ailse O'Fussers and her team of "lime gals", mindful of the inscription on the tomb of packman Christopher Duckworth above Haslingden, "loving his horses, by his horses loved"'.

There's no fulfilment without love. For my mother, all those miles, all those maps, all those dementing photographs were fuelled by love – love of life, love of place, love of the past, love of the present. With the mist swirling in, the clouds squatting on your head and my mother pointing over a sea of bog-cotton and saying brightly 'let's just . . .' it was sometimes hard to feel the love. Occasionally, even for my mother, it was love through clenched teeth and raw cheeks. Love isn't always easy. I learned that from her. I also learned from all those miles and all those maps that even when there are no clouds in the sky, up Stoodley it's likely raining.

29

LOST, FOUND, LOST

IN THE NOT-SO-GRAND house, catastrophe had a pattern. Rainy day, everything miserable, no catastrophe. Sunny day, everything happy, catastrophe. God has his little ways.

Catastrophe was usually dog- or horse-related. Dog-related was usually dog violence of some form – dog-on-dog, dog-on-human, dog-on-duck, dog-under-car, that kind of thing. Sometimes it was immediately dog-terminal, sometimes termination took a little longer. We once had a sheep-killing dog. Immediate termination. In most people's opinion Brock wasn't terminal quickly enough. Horse-related catastrophe was usually carelessness or foolhardiness and always involved blood, the blood more spectacular, so it often turned out, than the injury. But when real catastrophe came, the kind that can still stun you years later, the day was neither sunny nor particularly happy. It was just a day. November. Cold. Dank. Dark by half-past three.

It was my turn to walk up to the yard and catch from the field Mr. Not-So-Crazy and a dainty mare we had on trial to buy. The drill was familiar: pop them in their stables, rug them up and feed them, and then feed the Kicker who, with Miss Pretty and other assorted shaggy ponies in our collection, lived out all year. I was halfway over the meadow when I heard hoofbeats trotting up the lane beyond the bigger field in which the ponies grazed. I ran, calling the name of the Kicker, that keenest of escapees. When I got into the yard, there he was, standing by the field gate. He wasn't alone. I could see the shape of Miss Pretty, also waiting for her tea. I didn't look further. If the Kicker wasn't out, none of them would be out.

The stables were ready: clean, sweet-smelling, banked high with straw, haynets hanging, water-buckets in the corner so I headed straight for the feed-room. Feeding horses is both science and art. Without being fancy, my mother studied the science and intuited the art, the result being a chart detailing which pony should get what. I was following the chart, measuring bran, oats and barley, sugarbeet, treacle and vinegar when I heard slow hoofbeats coming up the stable drive. Still clutching the bran scoop I ran out. Through the gloom and the drizzle appeared the mare we had on trial. She walked straight into her stable. I ran and bolted the door, then, heart not yet really catapulting, I ran over the yard and through the field gate, pushing between the ponies still standing there, through the mud, over the stream and there it was: the gate onto the lane, the gate that was never used, its hinges never oiled, its weedy carpet never touched, there it was, wide open. Even in the dark I could see tyre marks. Somebody in a car, taking fright at the narrowing lane and the overgrowth on each side, had trampled the weedy carpet, manhandled the gate open, done a u-turn and left the gate gaping. The gate-crashers may have encouraged the ponies or they may not even have seen them. Didn't matter now. The only thing that mattered was that whilst the Kicker and Miss Pretty had remained behind, it was likely that two horses and one pony had gone through. Only one horse had returned.

There being no telephone in the stable-yard, and I wasn't yet thinking catastrophe, I pulled the gate shut as best I could and continued running up the lane, panting, calling, calling, panting, calling. The lane is steep, dividing at the top. To the right, round a sharp bend, you get up to the main road. To the left, more track-like, you pass cottages and the home farm. Riding out, we nearly always went left. That was the way up to the moor. Surely the horses would have gone left. I went left. No sign along the track so I ran into the farmyard. Now my heart was sinking, still not catastrophe sinking, more sinking at having to ask Mr. S., as surly and harsh as the land he farmed, for help. His dogs roared and pulled on their chains. He was at the door before I reached it. I was garbled. He'd heard nothing, he said. Dogs hadn't barked until I came. He went inside, grabbed his cap, shouted at the dogs and we set off together still on foot. Without speaking he headed for the main road and now my heart was catapulting from more than the running. Up at the main road we turned left because we could see through the darkness and the drizzle that a car, facing away from us, had stopped. Mr. Not-So-Crazy lay on the side of the road. He was completely unmarked but Mr. S. and I both knew he was dead. The couple from the car were distraught. They hadn't seen him, they said, they just hadn't seen him, hadn't seen him at all and there had been two horses, they said, this one on the outside. The horses had been facing the car, they said. In other words the horses, knowing it was teatime, had turned round and were heading home.

'You get back, get your mother,' Mr. S. said to me. 'I'll see to this.'

And now the evening took on that strange other-worldliness of catastrophe. Running back down the lane, I watched myself as though through a camera lens. I shivered the awful horror-film shiver of knowing something terrible that at that moment nobody else knew. I couldn't believe it was real. 'No no no no' I repeated as I ran and then, along with my panting and my 'no no no' I heard noise from the stable yard. A sister was shouting. I ran faster. She carried on shouting. When I reached the yard she was standing by the stable-door I'd bolted about ten minutes earlier and still, still she was shouting. I unbolted the door and went in. The mare who had returned, the mare we had on trial, was standing in the corner, her head thrust so deep into her water-bucket I thought she was drowning. 'Steady, steady,' is what every horse-person says. 'Steady, steady.' She couldn't steady because when she raised her head it was clear that a spike, perhaps from a fence, perhaps something from the car, had gone through the bottom of her jaw, through and out. The wound was vicious but clean. The water in the bucket was red. The sister ran back over the meadow to alert the household.

In the dark and the drizzle the full panoply of catastrophe unfolded: the vet for the wounded, the knacker for the dead, the police for the missing. Nobody wailed or shrieked. The catastrophe was too big for that. Much later, my mother gently sent me home. My father was waiting. He gave me brandy. Nanny had run a bath. Nobody uttered one word of blame. They didn't have to. 'If only I'd gone up to the stables a quarter of an hour earlier.' 'If only I hadn't seen the Kicker in the field.' 'If only I'd run faster up the lane.' If only, if only. The two saddest words in the English language.

That night I learned that grief is different from crying. Crying is what you do, and not always at once. Crying can be wild and over-whelming. You can't see how you'll ever stop. You do stop. Nobody cries forever. Grief is the stone in your throat that sits undigested. Grief never goes away. Eventually it beds in and becomes part of you. I also learned that what I'd previously labelled catastrophes were minor inconveniences. Real catastrophe was far beyond the destruction of lawn by small hooves, far beyond being late for Mass, far beyond even Brock killing a dozen ducks. Real catastrophe wasn't a series of things that went wrong and could be put right. Real catastrophe was indelible. You couldn't anticipate it. You couldn't control it. It rolled in, rolled on, and though time might pass, it never rolled away.

We lost the dainty mare. All the money and veterinary expertise in the world couldn't save her. The missing pony, so small and black he seemed destined for death in the dark, we found unhurt two days later in a field some miles away. The other ponies seemed unsurprised by his return. If they mourned the other gaps in their ranks, the mourning was quiet, the gaps accepted. Horses don't suffer from 'if only'.

For us, the gaps remained raw. Some days I might have stopped riding altogether. Yet that early revelation about a rider being something you were, not something you did, kept the riding flame alight. Even so, it was many many months before we raised our heads. 'Onwards,' said my mother when she thought we were ready. Onwards we went.

Our first 'onwards' was to buy a pony from Leicestershire, her hind quarters flat as that county. Unloaded from the lorry she was aghast. Hills! Ridden out for the first time, she was more aghast. Nothing but hills! That's the deal, we said. Take it or leave it. Being good-natured, she took it and developed a surprisingly agile turn of foot though she never truly loved it. What she loved was hunting, where she was so impeccably behaved we once lent her to a nonagenarian blind horseman for a final day with the hounds. Keenly, carefully, she took him over the country, this old man, his seat still perfect, his faith commendable. Occasionally we'd shout 'ditch!' or 'hedge' or 'fence' and he'd nod, balancing himself as the pony carried him over. I'm sure the old man was really hoping to die that day, and given his age, his blindness, a keen pony and hounds running full tilt, it was a reasonable hope. For the pony's sake we were glad it remained just that.

She had come with glowing recommendations from past owners; a sensible purchase. Against all her own advice, my mother purchased another, not from Leicestershire and this time on instinct. We were looking for a fifteen hand bay gelding, already broken, tried and tested so when unexpectedly presented with a 14.2hh mare, colour vague under the mud, clearly unbroken and neither tried nor tested at anything at all, we said no. To be polite, we remained with this mare-we-didn't-want whilst the farmer quite unnecessarily went to fetch a certificate to do with a foal she'd had. The mare was restive so my mother took her for a walk. When they returned, my mother said 'we'll have her' and we did.

'What happened on the walk?' I asked. We were standing back after washing the mare, a little disconcerted to find that, as suspected but rather dreaded, she was chestnut – a chestnut mare! Traditionally a nightmare! My mother began to separate the strands of the mare's tail. 'She walked so well,' my mother said. 'She was so unsettled and she knew nothing, but still she walked so well.' After a pause, 'we walked well together'.

If lucky, living creatures meet at least one other living creature who brings out the best in each. For humans, it's sometimes other humans. More often, it's something non-human: a brute caring for a songbird, the songbird singing for the brute; the hard man thirled to his dog, the hard dog thirled to his man; the awkward child finding solace in a rat, the rat unjudging of the awkward child. My mother and this little chestnut mare had this reciprocity. For them the root was trust.

The trust that grew between them wasn't magic. Not at all. The trust was based on hours and hours of training during which the little mare learned not to say 'no' because my mother wouldn't ask the impossible, and my mother learned that the little mare never would say no, so never to ask the impossible. My mother veered pretty near the edge though. In pursuit of those packhorse trails, along with climbing and scrambling, she asked the mare to tiptoe along precipices, navigate steps, plough through mud, straddle ditches, wade under waterfalls, and hop over or squeeze under bridges that were distinctly not to be hopped over or squeezed under. During the bi-annual Vienna to Budapest horse-race – my mother, in her element, comprised one half of the two-woman British team – the mare boarded a leaky raft of roughly-bound planks to cross the Danube. She learned to go at top speed, at steady speed, at no speed at all; to wait in the wind while my mother took all those maddening research photographs; to shuffle about helping with gates when hounds were running; to ignore things that banged and to carry things that flapped. When my mother had no alternative but to dismount, the mare responded by edging up to anything with height so that my mother who, despite her neat figure and light weight, had less bounce than a cannon ball, could climb back on. They made an ears-pricked, up-and-away pair, both preferring fast to slow, the front to the back, the 'let's go' to the 'shall we go'. In moments of poor visibility my mother was wont to call out 'we need to keep the trig point to the north', an instruction about as useful as a paper map to a robin. She trusted the mare to get her home.

One chink in the armour. As chickens were to my mother, so pigs were to the mare. One day, perhaps fifteen miles from home and with no way round, our way was blocked by a supine Large White sow. Lying sideways on, the sow took up the whole path, nose slightly squashed against one bank, tail slightly squashed against the other. The mare was utterly affronted. Snort snort. Tail up. Nose up. Piaffe. The sow regarded this cartoon outrage impassively, correctly calculating that a piaffing horse presented no threat whatsoever. She grunted her dismissal, shifted her bulk to scratch an itch, settled back down and blinked, her two front legs and one back leg sticking out like the legs on a milking stool, her fourth leg tucked up at a jaunty angle. Like all pigs, she seemed to be smiling.

'Well,' said my mother as the mare pranced and trembled and the pig smiled and smiled, 'here's a thing.' She settled the mare facing the pig. 'Now,' said my mother. 'Forward.' A moment's hesitation, a moment's indecision, then blowing hard, the mare sprang into a smart trot. Roughly eight or nine feet away from the pig she stopped dead. We prepared for a stand-off, for a first absolute 'no' by the mare who never said no. My mother frowned. 'We might have to move the pig.'

Even as she spoke the mare leapt, forging into the air like Pegasus, front legs tucked well in, back legs thrusting up, over and out until, unable to keep tucked any longer, she stretched her front legs and reached for the ground as far beyond the sow as she could manage. It was the biggest leap I'd ever seen. My mother did well to stay on. The sow, momentarily startled by the shadow passing over her, raised her head and I, on the non-pig-hating Leicestershire pony, slithered past. By the time I reached my mother, the mare had recovered herself and my mother had resettled in the saddle. 'Pigs,' my mother said in just the tone of voice I imagined the mare might use. 'They're much better as bacon.' We laughed and carried on, but my mother was upset with herself. She should never have doubted the mare. I doubt she ever doubted her again.

The weather always unhelpful, it was hard to find the best questing garments. You needed to be warm, but not too warm; dry without being hampered. Rootling about in a scullery drawer one freezing winter's morning, my mother felt something soft and furry. She pulled, and out slid a black balaclava. She slipped it on. We were aghast. She resembled one of those round-topped Halma pegs. Unbothered, she declared it the find of the year, crammed it under her crashcap and was not to be parted from it again. Gifts of other forms of warmth and protection were met with polite but rejecting thanks. None came up to balaclava standard.

Doing some rootling myself after my mother's death, I found the balaclava in a coat pocket. Still as horrible as it had always been, it seemed destined for the bin, except as it vanished beneath the tealeaves and banana skins I found myself weeping for my mother all over again. I hadn't expected to cry over a balaclava. Not knowing quite what to do, I fished the thing out, washed it and put it in a drawer. In all my letting go, what a thing to keep.

Above the water-troughs in Not-So-Grand house's stable yard are inscribed the names of all the horses whose lives entwined with ours: the discards and the chosen; the sensible and the flighty; the loved dearly and the loved not-quite-so-dearly; the ill-tempered and the sweet-tempered; the short-lived and the long-lived; those whose manes were easily plaited, those whose manes made only potatoes. My mother's little chestnut, the mare she loved above all others, takes pride of place. I sometimes trace the names or stand in the chestnut mare's empty stable listening to the rain flooding the gutter pipe. I want to think great thoughts about what we had, what we did, how it was. There are no great thoughts. Just an awful ache.

30

COMING OUT

IN 1976, THE term 'coming out' still meant regular party appearances for the London social season and, almost impossible now to believe, being part of the parade of society girls at the annual Queen Charlotte's Ball. Before the 1950s, the Ball, instigated by George III in 1780 to honour his wife's birthday, was held at Buckingham Palace, each debutante presented to the monarch. During the 1950s, after the late queen declared the thing too nonsensical, QCB moved from Buckingham Palace to the Grosvenor House hotel. In the absence of the monarch and completely in keeping with the original founder's madness, debutantes now curtsied to a cake.

I was one of those curtseying girls. At bottom, the point of 'coming out' was to find a husband. At least that was certainly the point for most fathers who, through cautionary tales shared at their clubs, were suddenly alive to the possible pursuit of their daughters by Boys Who Were Not Remotely Suitable. My father ignored the alarm. After years at convent schools, so far as he was aware his daughters knew very few boys and those we did know were nearly all relations. Secondly, we lived in Lancashire, a county beaten in unfashionability only by, say, Nottinghamshire. Unsuitable suitors were unlikely to beat any kind of path to our door. Some consternation when a boy had to be found as my Queen Charlotte's escort. From the choice of relations, a reluctant cousin was eventually commandeered. Handsome and dashing, Reluctant Cousin may also have been witty. Since he never spoke to me I can't vouch for that.

My mother did try to raise some interest in the 'coming out' business. We bought expensive off-white material for the regulation QCB white-white dress. 'They can't really mean white as in white-white,' my mother said. 'It must be a misprint.' With my father's enthusiastic approval she looked out some of my great-grandmother's fine antique lace for embellishment. The 1976 official debutante photographs tell the story. The off-white just about blends in with everybody else's white-white. The antique lace, despite many careful washings, looks pilfered from Miss Havisham's coffin. 1976 was the last Queen Charlotte's Ball. Drug-taking and 'loucheness' were blamed. Encased in what Eldest Sister christened 'corpse-lace', I was disappointed to experience neither.

After the Ball, invitations arrived, usually from people I didn't know but whose fathers my father knew. Once the connection was established, the fathers seemed surprised to find my father had daughters – he'd never said. Whatever the connection, the invitations were unstoppable. I was asked for drinks, for dances, for weekends including dances. I was asked to assorted post-dance lunches in country piles in Gloucestershire or Oxfordshire or Hampshire or Leicestershire. With some trepidation and truly terrible clothes I accepted them all. If I tried hard enough, surely I could feel at home in the world of Laura Ashley spriggy skirts, borrowed pearls, Gucci shoes, huskies (jackets not dogs), sleeveless puffas and striped shirts? What was not to like about flats in London's SWs, your bottom cheaply scratched by Izal loo paper and your hands expensively scented with Floris soap? Did it really matter if, in conversation, the far North meant Islington? I felt ready to find my place in the world of Caroline and her Hooray Henry made famous by Ann Barr and Peter York in *The Sloane Ranger's Handbook*.

And let's be truthful: that world was magnificent, the country piles magnificent, the parties magnificent, the hangovers magnificent, everything magnificent. At one coming-of-age magnificence the wine had been specially bottled and labelled twenty-one years before. At another, a fancy-dress affair, my whole monthly salary went to a theatrical costumier. Avoiding any risk of more corpse-lace, for the highland balls I went the full Meg March (*Little Women*) and begged and borrowed enough dresses to see me through. If champagne befuddled any memory of dancing partners, I could find their names scrawled on the dance-cards, tasselled pencil still attached. Inspecting the dance-cards, my father was hopeful. Surely amid all this tartan McFlummery there'd be a husband?

It wasn't a vain hope. On paper, my Sloane Ranger credentials were impeccable: birth, school, after-school, and I did shop at Laura Ashley. To top it off, like the then Diana Spencer, the *ne plus ultra* Sloane, I shared a flat in SW10. Yet however hard I tried, there was a problem. Sloanery was essentially home-counties manor-houses and Yorkshire palaces, buttery sunshine and anyone-for-tennis. To many of my friends it came as naturally as loving Jane Austen. Alas, love Austen as I did, I remained a Bronte girl. Buttery sunshine turned me puce. Tennis? A humiliation. Not only that, but dark, unpretty and constitutionally allergic to 'bright young things', the Not-So-Grand house wasn't having any truck with this southern Sloanery conceit. When Sloane friends came to stay or were billeted with us in house-parties for dances miles away, it wailed and sulked with special fervour, shorting their hairdryers and encouraging the rain to drip with spiteful malevolence through the roofs of any Sloaney convertible. Add to these infelicities my father's jousting, my mother's marmalade habit and, until that terminal needle, Brock, and I realised then, as I'd always really known, that I could roll myself in Laura Ashley wallpaper and hang Gucci shoes from my ears but the only Sloane success I'd achieve would be of the more disturbing kind.

As the Sloane Ranger handbook astutely observes, between 'coming out' and marrying Sloaney Henry, it's part of Sloaney lore that Sloaney Caroline meets the unSloaney world. If she's not careful, that unSloaney world tips her into a 'fat and emotionally unbalanced'[*] phase from which she may or may not recover. I came out, was not careful and tipped, so I did the only thing I could think of: shoved all my Laura Ashley into the dustbin and slunk back to the proper north. After a month or two my father glanced up from *The Times* and asked in apparent surprise, 'Have you been here long?'

A quick panic. 'I'm just off.'

'Off? Where to?'

There was an article about India, cricket I think, on the back of the newspaper. 'India,' I said.

'Good,' said my father, and so it was set.

On departure day, April Fool's Day as it happens, I found my mother in the kitchen. 'Will you be back for lunch?' she asked, one eye glued to the horses' linseed, the other to a map. In the library, my father glanced up momentarily. 'Whatever happens, don't ask me for money.'

Both responses being entirely, reassuringly, familiar, I paid a last visit to the attic loo, hauled my rucksack onto my back, and left.

Years later, I found my letters from India in a drawer in my mother's sitting room. Flicking through, I could see that although in essential facts my letters were true, their resolutely cheerful tone was false. Always mindful that being unhappy is dull and that being dull is the worst sin of all, I suppose I wrote the letters I thought my parents would want me to write. Those thin blue aerograms are full of adventures and mishaps, alarms and excursions. They're the letters of the happy Sloane-In-India. Since my happiness was as forced as my Sloanery, they're not good letters. Re-reading them, I wondered whether my parents had found them as disappointing then as I did now.

Over supper one evening, a decade or so after my mother's death, I asked my father about those letters. With either honesty or tact (I

* Barr, A. and Yorke, P., 1982, *The Official Sloane Ranger Handbook*, Ebury Press, p. 110

incline to the former) he said he couldn't remember reading them. 'I think we thought you were happy,' he said, pouring more wine, and then, out of the blue, 'Do you think your mother was happy?'

As with his asking about being a good father, this question was entirely unexpected. I probably gaped. 'I don't know,' I said. 'I don't think anybody knows much about anybody else's happiness.' It wasn't the answer he wanted. It would have been kinder to lie.

I don't remember what we spoke about after that because 'happiness' sent me back to an afternoon in 1991. I'd just had my third baby and my mother, seeing me struggle, was trying to advise me, without using any advisory words, that three children was enough. I caught her drift and agreed, commiserating over the disappointment that she, an obedient Catholic, must have felt in the Humanae Vitae summer of 1968 when, with the contraceptive pill fast establishing itself, Pope Paul didn't relax the 1930s edict that 'artificial' birth control was 'intrinsically evil'. Not a happy outcome, I sympathised, for somebody who already had six children.

My mother didn't mince her words. Even had the pope allowed the pill, she'd never have taken it. And then, without pause or hint of irony, 'contraception makes you fat,' she declared.

'Like Sloanery,' I said. She looked puzzled, then her face cleared and for just a moment we seemed poised for some of those confidences we'd never shared in the bone-shaker Land Rover or whilst ploughing those miles in search of the past, confidences that might have helped me answer my father's happiness question with more certainty. Perhaps the baby cried. Perhaps the telephone rang. At any rate, my mother stood up. 'Well,' she said, 'at least I avoided that.' Did she mean fatness or Sloanery? Perhaps she meant both.

When my father had gone to bed, I removed all my Indian letters from the desk and put them in a bag for burning. Then I went upstairs to find that off-white dress. I shook off its tissue paper. The corpse-lace had been removed. Plain, it was beautiful as a pearl. Also surprisingly, almost impossibly, narrow. Even before my 'fat and emotionally unbalanced' phase, had I ever really been that thin? I was tempted to try it on. If I could do it up, that would make me as happy as my mother had been when she slipped easily into her wedding dress for a dinner to celebrate her and my father's twenty-fifth wedding anniversary. And then it struck me. Nobody who has been unhappy in their marriage wants to put on their wedding dress again. I should have woken my father to tell him. I didn't, so perhaps he never knew.

31

HEFTED

I FOLLOWED MY letters from India home eventually, with a text-book Unsuitable Boy and a disappointment. Usually, people who went to India fat came back thin. In my case, the culinary foibles of the Not-So-Grand house had triumphed once again. Though I cracked my pelvis falling off a racehorse, caught fleas sharing a sleeping bag with mice and was nearly killed by an elephant, my stomach remained untroubled. This made me the only person I knew, or anybody seemed to know, who'd returned from a third-class Indian experience exactly the same shape as when they left.

Over Unsuitable Boy, I'd like to say 'Reader, I married him'. I didn't. Contrary to my father's predictions, he did, though, find his way to Burnley. There he was at Burnley Central Station, a tall, dark Canadian in top-to-toe flowing orange robes. What the Not-So-Grand house and household, and particularly my father, would make of this ardent follower of the Bhagwan Shree Rajnesh fresh from the ashram in Pune, I wasn't sure. A new strategy would be needed. But my father was charmed; my mother was charmed. The only person not charmed was me, and when Unsuitable Boy suggested we join together in the 'eternal Om of matrimony' or somesuch, I devised a strategy of my own.

'There's an old Lancashire tradition,' I said, or words to similar effect, 'that if you ask somebody to marry you and they refuse, you have to leave right that second.'

He didn't believe me.

'It's to do with packhorses,' I explained, and blessing my mother, employed all the language of Ailse O'Fussers and the 'lime gals'. I wonder if it's the only instance of a marriage refusal through broadgates and narrowgates, cauls and causeys, cloughs and clunters, snickets and spandrels.

He was baffled.

'You don't need to understand the jargon,' I reassured. 'You only need to understand that I should really leave you on the moor, but if you get in the car now I'll take you to the station.'

'The station? It's the middle of the night!'

'Station or moor?'

He got into the car. I dumped him at the station and told him to wait for the milk train. 'Milk train? I've never heard of a milk train.' His orange robes offered little protection against the dawn chill. No matter. I gathered myself into my father's daughter. 'Really,' I said, and with that Exocet zinger I left him.

Back home everybody was disappointed. Six unmarried daughters was beginning to worry my father. What, he asked testily, was the matter with orange? My mother remarked that the milk train had been abolished decades before. Once the disappointment had abated, the slippery slope reasserted itself. 'I hope he signed the Book?'

My father meant the Visitors Book, a major slippery slope concern. Every visitor must sign. Come fire or nuclear attack, you must still sign. Saving the Visitors Book came way above saving a child or even an animal. The Book lived by the front door, well within a saving grasp, and even amid the causeys, cloughs and clunters I hadn't forgotten. 'Of course,' I said. With my father's grunt, the orange man was history.

Some years later, post-honeymoon with a less orange man, no longer fat and somewhat rebalanced, I drove from my new home in Scotland to the Not-So-Grand house to collect my dog – not Brock, long dead by then, a different dog, a non-demon dog. My father was waiting at the top of the drive, his face set. He had my dog with him. Before I could move, my father whisked open the passenger door and popped the dog in. 'Don't get out,' he said. 'I know you and this place. You're like a hefted sheep. If you come in you'll never leave.'

I drove away but like a hefted sheep I never really did leave. Though I've lived well over half my life elsewhere when I say 'I'm going home' I mean the Not-So-Grand house halfway up the hill in the mouth of the gorge, moors above, Burnley below. Still leaking like a drain in the rain, still howling like a banshee in the wind, the house is further down the slippery slope than it was. Like the mines and the mills one day it will fall off the end. Yet that doesn't make it easier to let go, perhaps because of the life that was lived there, perhaps because these days, for tiny estates like my father's, though male primogeniture is a serious matter it's almost impossible to take seriously.

And it feels so random. Biological sex may be determined at fertilisation but it's just luck who gets to stay and who has to leave. If only the cap I wore when I ran away had turned me into a boy! Then there'd be no letting go for me to do. But the cap remained unmagical so I have had to accept what's been ordained.

I can still see my father standing at the top of the drive. He didn't wave. I didn't wave. As my dog and I left Burnley and the moors behind I thought, not for the first time, that if you're going to be hefted, it's luckier to be a sheep than a girl.

32

JULY 2024

'THE DASHWOODS ARE upon us' texted Fifth Sister. Sibling codes, unexplainable to outsiders, compress decades of complex family relationships into shorthand. Those four words from the sister who'd been living in the Not-So-Grand house with my father had me heading for my car.

My father had now been dead for nearly two years but despite knowing from birth that he was The Heir, Only Brother and his family were taking their time moving into the house and assuming the Towneley mantle. 'The Dashwoods are upon us' meant the moment had arrived. They're moving in on Monday, Fifth Sister said. Today was Friday.

Even when uncontested, the take-over by one sibling of a family house feels awkward. Everybody avoids the word 'hostile', but there are hostilities. Certain things - paintings, books, china, pieces of furniture - the gatherings of decades, mean more to some than to others. In our case, the gatherings were of centuries. There were also things of actual value, things of sentimental value and a lot of things sunk so far into disrepair they were only fit for the skip. As is the way with male primogeniture, all the valuable things now belonged to Only Brother. Only the sentimental things were still the sisters' domain. Before the skip was ordered, there needed to be a final sentimental sifting.

It was clear when I managed to push open the front door that I hadn't absolutely understood the code. In addition to sentimental things lined up for inspection – home-made presents, inconsequential knick-knacks, photograph albums, childhood toys – the entire contents of cupboards, chests, sideboards, closets and storerooms, some of the contents last seeing daylight half a century ago, had been emptied out, along with an accumulation of dead creatures and fifty years of dust. Picking my way carefully through the hall, down the passage and into the back of the house I eventually found Fifth Sister in the schoolroom. Something tall, pale and rustly lurked behind her. Fifth Sister stepped backwards. Loud popping. 'I think I have enough bubble wrap,' she said. She was holding the dreadful old stockpot. It was then I realised my mistake. There would be no sifting: Fifth Sister and I were to embark on a full-scale, indiscriminate rescue mission.

And so we began. We wrapped jugs with no spouts, teapots with no handles, seven coffee-cups with five saucers, four or five sets of tea things, all delicate, all hand-painted, but no cup without a chip and some so hopelessly glued together no tea could possibly remain inside. We wrapped soup-bowls unfit for soup; fruit bowls unfit for fruit, sugar bowls whose fragile flower covers, despite obvious care, were missing petals and stems. We wrapped the hat bit of a cheese hat. We wrapped titchy tiny individual jam and honeypots from the most elegant breakfast set, probably last used in the 1930s, jam and honey still inside, crystallised to rock.

'Shall I try and get it out?'

Fifth Sister was appalled. 'NO!'

We wrapped frying pans with no grips, saucepans with no lids, kitchen implements so out-dated their function was a mystery. We wrapped broken soup tureens, cracked plates, shards of vases, four and a half ramekins and a bowl in three bits. We wrapped the last remaining glass of a once exquisite set together with six glasses my mother got from the garage with her Green Shield stamps. We wrapped knives with no forks, forks with no knives. We wrapped the 'unbreakable' picnic stuff much of it broken. We wrapped the rusted mouli last used by Nanny, the round wooden butter mould which for years stamped a sparrowhawk on every pat of butter that went into the dining room, and all the cookbooks, some without covers, most stained beyond reading by fingers long dead. Every time I held something up – a crumbling mustard pot, a corroded salt cellar – and mouthed 'skip?' Fifth Sister threw more bubble wrap, so on we went. In the end we'd have wrapped the dust had it settled long enough.

And where was The Saved, as we might call it, to go? Fifth Sister was ready for that. She was moving to a farmhouse on a hill further down the gorge. The farmhouse had a big barn whose roof boasted only one or two holes, perhaps three. 'In there, of course,' she said. As always in moments of crisis, there was a problem. Part of the lane leading to the farmhouse had been washed away. The camber was lethal. You could tackle it on a horse but no reasonable person would attempt it in a car. Fifth Sister is not a reasonable person so we hitched an open trailer to her car and in the manner of a First World War ambulance, filled it with the broken and the wrecked, the damaged and the shattered.

It took us four journeys, each journey more tilted than the last as the wheels spun and car and trailer listed drunkenly towards the drop into the bottom of the valley. 'Hold tight!' Fifth Sister and I shouted uselessly at each other. The Saved, jolted from their long sleep into this strangely lopsided mission of mercy, lurched and bounced.

When all was done, car recovering, trailer tyres cooling, us with a restorative stiff drink, Fifth Sister and I trailed round the Not-So-Grand house in silence. Despite the volume of stuff we'd removed, the place was still full of stuff. It was, nonetheless, a melancholy farewell tour, particularly the room in which we had sat with my father as he died, the room in which I had felt the first chills of being a visitor. Damp marbled the walls. The window frames were rotting. The fireplace which, in my mother's time, had burned hot and fierce with Mrs N.'s spills, was smudged with grime fallen down the chimney. The chair at the escritoire at which my father had sat every evening to pray was untidily pushed to one side. Unaccountably, at least to me, my great-grandmother's wooden bed with its leaden mattress had vanished. Enough, I thought. Let go. Time for the new.

Except Monday came and no Dashwoods. And many Mondays after, still none. At the time of writing, the Not-So-Grand house sits waiting, perhaps in vain. Yet it won't kill me, as you may remember my cousin warned it might. It won't because whilst the Not-So-Grand house of my childhood is gone, its meaningful life abandoned, its rooms given over to echoes and its complaints for the most part unheard, the valleyed gorge with its streams and cloughs will remain. The battered crags and tumbled boulders will remain. And my final letting go will not be a letting go at all because underneath the scrub grass and peaty softness, somewhere between the squelch and the firmer going, welcomed, absorbed, folded in, will be what remains of me.

BIBLIOGRAPHY

Burnley Express, *Images of Burnley* (The Breedon Books Publishing Company, Derby, 1996).

Chapples, Leslie, *Noblesse Oblige: a Towneley chronicle of historical fact, marriage links and notable family associations* (Burnley & District Historical Society, Burnley, 1987).

Fort, Keith, *Burnley Since 1900: Ninety Years of Photographs* (Archive Publications in association with the *Lancashire Evening Telegraph*, Burnley, 1988).

Miller, A. P., *Memories of the Worsthorne Estate, Burnley, Lancashire from 1915 to 1997* (Unpublished).

Thornber, Titus, *Seen on the Packhorse Tracks* (The South Pennines Packhorse Trails Trust, Burnley, 2002).

BOOKS REFERENCED

Barr, Ann and Yorke, Peter, *The Official Sloane Ranger Handbook* (Ebury Press, London, 1982).

Browning, Robert, 'The Bishop Orders His Tomb at Saint Praxted's Church', *Dramatic Romances and Lyrics* (London, 1845).

MacDonald, George, *At the Back of the North Wind* (Strahan & Co., London, 1871).

Nield Chew, Doris, *A Venture in the Arts: The Mid-Pennine Association for the Arts 1966-1978* (Mid Pennine Arts).

Norland, *Employing a Norland Nanny* (https://www.norland.ac.uk/
employing-a-norland-nanny/)

Norman, Priscilla, *In The Way of Understanding* (Foxbury Press,
London, 1982).

Woolf, Virginia, 'The Life of John Mytton', *Vogue* (London, March
1926).

Worsthorne, Peregrine, *Tricks of Memory* (Weidenfeld & Nicolson,
London, 1993).

ACKNOWLEDGEMENTS

THIS MEMOIR OWES a lot to a lot of people, many of them dead. Dead but never forgotten. Of the living, so many I'd run out of space. But I'd particularly like to thank my uncle Charlie Fitzherbert for sharing my Fitzherbert grandfather's WWI diary and my cousin Maggie Fergusson for her beautiful piece in The Tablet (6 July 2019); my agent, Polly Halladay of Georgina Capel Associates, whose all-seeing eye never faltered; and Salt Publishing's Chris and Jen Hamilton-Emery, whose enthusiasm and care could move mountains.

To Steve Cook and David Swinburne of the Royal Literary Fund, a triple thank you for all the work you do, all the support you give and all the education programmes you enable. The RLF transforms lives. It's a privilege and a joy to be part of that transformation.

To Annie Tempest, friend, consummate professional and multi-talented artist, thank you so much for painting the covers, front and back. I love them.

And perhaps the biggest thank you to my husband William, whose patience and love have been sorely tried but never found wanting.

In Chapter 15, 'Staying Alive', I haven't included Roger Fitzherbert-

Brockholes, another of my Fitzherbert grandfather's brothers. Roger was killed in 1919, aged 28, whilst clearing mines from the Dvina River as part of the Archangel Campaign. RIP.

Katharine Grant

This book has been typeset by
SALT PUBLISHING LIMITED
using Neacademia, a font designed by Sergei Egorov for the
Rosetta Type Foundry in Czechia. It has been manufactured
using Holmen Book Cream 65gsm paper, and printed and
bound by Clays Limited in Bungay, Suffolk, Great Britain.

CROMER
GREAT BRITAIN
MMXXVI